Wishing you a

Christmas

from Peter Margery &

David.

We love you!

# Designs for Fashion Knitting

# Designs for Fashion Knitting

Barbara Jordan

B.T. Batsford Ltd London

*With particular thanks to: Margaret Thorpe, Margaret Brown, Barbara Davis, June Smith, and especially to Mrs Frances Williams*



First published 1985



ISBN 0 7134 4584 X

Typeset by Servis Filmsetting Ltd, Manchester
and printed in Great Britain by
Anchor Brendon Ltd, Tiptree, Essex
for the publishers
B.T. Batsford Ltd
4 Fitzhardinge Street
London W1H 0AH

# CONTENTS

# ABBREVIATIONS

| | |
|---|---|
| K | knit |
| P | purl |
| st(s) | stitch(es) |
| st st | stocking stitch |
| sl (st) | slip (stitch) |
| wrn | wool round needle |
| wf | wool forward |
| wb | wool back |
| psso | pass slip stitch over |
| tog | together |
| tbl | through back of loop(s) |
| inc | increase(ing) |
| dec | decrease(ing) |
| beg | begin(ning) |
| alt | alternate |
| rep | repeat(ed) |
| patt | pattern |
| incl | inclusive |
| in | inch(es) |
| cm | centimetre(s) |
| o | no stitches, times or rows |
| M1 | make one stitch |
| cont | continue |
| foll | following |
| rem | remaining |
| kw | knitwise |
| pw | purlwise |

# THE BASICS OF KNITTING

## Tension

Few knitters realise how important it is to check the tension of their knitting, yet this is the key to successful knitting and designing. If the tension is too loose by even half a stitch to 2cm ($\frac{13}{16}$in), a garment designed to measure 91cm (36in) could easily turn out to be 101cm (40in). Even worse, if the tension is too tight by half a stitch to 2cm ($\frac{13}{16}$in), the sweater you make to measure 91cm (36in) will in fact measure 83cm (33in), and be unwearable.

It is, therefore, essential that you check your tension before beginning to knit a garment, especially with all the different quality yarns on the market. Every knitter should knit up a tension square of at least 10cm (4in) before launching into a pattern, and, if unable to obtain the correct tension with the size of needle recommended, should experiment with larger or smaller needles until she can produce a sample swatch to the correct tension.

## Needle size

The chart below gives the old English equivalents to the metric needles, and the American sizing.

| Metric | English | American |
|---|---|---|
| 2 | 14 | 00 |
| 2¼ | 13 | 0 |
| 2¾ | 12 | 1 |
| 3 | 11 | 2 |
| 3¼ | 10 | 3 |
| 3¾ | 9 | 4 |
| 4 | 8 | 5 |
| 4½ | 7 | 6 |
| 5 | 6 | 7 |
| 5½ | 5 | 8 |
| 6 | 4 | 9 |
| 6½ | 3 | 10 |
| 7 | 2 | 10½ |

| Metric | English | American |
|---|---|---|
| 7½ | 1 | 11 |
| 8 | 0 | 12 |
| 9 | 00 | 13 |
| 10 | 000 | 15 |

## Casting on

There are a number of methods of casting on. The two-needle method is given below, and this is very satisfactory provided that the first row of knitting is worked into the backs of each cast-on stitch.

*The two-needle method*
Make a slip knot in the yarn and put it on to the needle. Hold this needle in your left hand and insert the other needle through the loop as for knitting; pass the yarn round the right-hand needle and draw it through the loop. Put this loop on the left needle and repeat the process for the number of stitches required.

## Increasing

*Increase one stitch* (usually abbreviated to 'inc 1')
Knit into the stitch and, before slipping it off the needle, knit again into the back of the loop.

*Make one stitch* (usually abbreviated to M1)
Knit into a loop of the previous row between the stitches.

*Wool round needle* (usually abbreviated to wrn)
*Between two purl stitches*, P the first stitch, bring the yarn over the right-hand needle and between both needles to the front; P the next stitch.
*Between a purl and a knit stitch*, bring the yarn forward between the needles, over the right-hand needle and between the needles to the front. P the next stitch.

## Decreasing

*Decrease one stitch* (usually abbreviated to 'dec 1')
K or P the first two stitches on the left-hand needle together.

## Buttons

Knitted buttons can be a feature of a garment, as well as, if required, being a perfect match. They are made by knitting two squares in stocking stitch or reverse stocking stitch, then oversewing the edges of the squares together and putting some wool stuffing in the centre (making sure to use enough stuffing to give a firm finish). Alternatively, cast on enough stitches to measure rather more than the diameter of the size button needed, and knit a square in stocking stitch for each button required. Sew a running thread all round the square and draw up over stuffing of matching yarn.

## Buttonholes

*Horizontal buttonholes*

These are made by casting off the required number of stitches and then casting on the same number above the cast-off stitches on the subsequent row.

*Vertical buttonholes*

These are made by turning when the position of the buttonhole is reached, and working on the first section of stitches only until the desired depth of the buttonhole has been reached. Then return to the second set of stitches and work to match the first set. When both sets have been worked, knit across all stitches.

Very small buttonholes can be made by working two stitches together, then bringing the yarn round needle before the next stitch.

## Pockets

*Patch pockets*

These pockets can easily be made by knitting a square or other shape and stitching it on to the garment in the required position.

*Horizontal pockets*

Make the pocket lining in stocking stitch to the size and shape of the pocket, then leave the stitches of the lining on a spare needle. Work the main fabric of the garment to seven rows before the level of the pocket top, ending on a right side row, then work six rows in rib or garter stitch across the pocket top stitches. On the next row cast off the pocket top stitches, working the remainder of the row in pattern, then work the following row in pattern to within one stitch of the pocket top.

Insert the pocket lining by knitting the next stitch of the main fabric together with the first stitch of the pocket lining, working across the pocket lining stitches in pattern to the last stitch but one, then working that stitch together with the next stitch of the main fabric. Continue as normal with the body of the garment, and slip stitch the pocket lining into position when making up.

### *Vertical pockets*

This kind must be made so that the hand can be inserted towards the centre front of the garment, and thus sufficient room must be left in the front of the garment to allow for this.

Having decided on the size of the pocket required, make the lining in stocking stitch and cast off the lining stitches. Work the main fabric of the garment to the position of the pocket, ending on a wrong side row, then, on the next row, work to the position of the pocket opening. Turn and work each side of the pocket opening separately until the desired depth has been completed, ending on a wrong side row. Now work across both sets of stitches.

When making up the garment, pick up the stitches along the edge of the pocket and work in rib or garter stitch, and, with the right side of the lining facing the wrong side of the garment, slip stitch the lining into position.

## Making up

The making up of the garment is extremely important, and a well-knitted garment can be ruined if insufficient attention is paid to its assembly.

First block the pieces of the garment by pinning them out to measurements on an ironing board or blanket. Read the pressing instructions on the ballband and, where appropriate, press the blocked pieces, avoiding the ribbing. Next join the seams of the garment by one of the following methods.

### *Oversewing*

Use yarn to match the garment and place the two pieces to be joined together with right sides facing. Oversew the edge stitches, matching stitch for stitch where possible.

### *Edge to edge method*

This can only be done when the edges are very neat. Hold both pieces flat with the edges meeting and the right sides facing the worker. Join with a lacing stitch, taking one loop from each side alternately. This should only be done in the same yarn as that of the main fabric.

### *Backstitch method*

This is most satisfactory for uneven edges. Place the right sides of both pieces together and backstitch firmly 12.5mm (½in) from the edge. Press the seam open where possible.

# DESIGNING A SWEATER

In order to write, and then knit, your own designs, you will need the following basic equipment: a ruler, a soft pencil, a rubber, yarn, knitting needles and imperial graph paper.

Now decide on the stitch you wish to use. There are many books of knitting stitch variations available, and you should use one of these to choose a stitch that complements your yarn. You must begin by knitting up a tension square, and you can use this to see what your chosen stitch looks like in the yarn you intend to use, and also to discover whether the stitch is easy or difficult to knit.

**Stitch tension**

You cannot begin to design your pattern until you have taken both row and stitch tension from your tension square; the tension should be measured without stretching the stitch sample. Once you have discovered the stitch tension you will be able to decide how many stitches you need for the body of the garment. Thus if you have a stitch tension of, say, 20 stitches to 10cm (4in), you know that for every centimetre in width you need, you must cast on 2 stitches (5 stitches for every inch). If you are designing an 86cm (34in) sweater, therefore, you will need to cast on enough stitches to measure approximately 46cm (18in) across both back and front, as you should always allow about 5cm (2in) extra across the bust for ease of movement. Thus a tension of 20 sts to 10cm (4in) would result in a requirement of at least 90 sts on each back and front to make a garment to fit an 86cm (34in) bust.

Before finally deciding on the number of stitches needed for any part of the garment you will also need to ensure that the stitch pattern you have chosen will fit into the total number of stitches to be worked. Your 86cm (34in) sweater does not have to measure 91cm (36in) exactly; if you want it to be close fitting, it could measure 90cm (35½in); if you want it to be loose it could be 97, 99 or even 101cm (38, 39 or 40in). Thus you have some room to manoeuvre when trying to fit in a stitch repeat, and if in our example the tension of 2 stitches to 1cm ($\frac{3}{8}$in) was obtained over an 8 stitch pattern, the back of the 86cm (34in) garment could be worked over 96, 104 or even 88 stitches, depending on how tight or loose you wanted the garment to be.

Having decided on the number of stitches, these should be marked along the bottom of the graph paper, as on Chart 1, and you should turn your attention to row tension.

### Row tension

Here again there are two considerations: the desired length of the garment and the number of rows in the stitch pattern. You should try to reach the last pattern row immediately before any shaping, i.e. before armhole, shoulder and, if possible, neck shaping. Having reconciled these two criteria, mark the number of rows to be worked on the graph paper. You now have the basic proportions of your sweater, and have only to add the shapings.

### Drop-shoulder jumper

By far the easiest sweater to design is the drop-shoulder jumper shown in Chart 1, as this requires no shaping other than that of the front neck. This can be done quite easily with the help of the measurement chart shown on p. 16. Having ascertained the size of the curve by deciding on the measurement of the back neck (measured in stitches) and that of the neck drop (measured in rows), draw a curve at the neck of the garment on your graph paper. You will be able to work out the usual measurements applied to neck shaping from the measurement chart, but you can vary these dimensions if you want a neckline other than a plain round neck, although you should not make any neckline smaller than that suggested in the chart.

There is no need for any shaping of the shoulders or back neck, other than to leave the back neck stitches on a stitch holder and pick them up when working the neckband. The back of the drop-shoulder sweater is therefore merely a knitted rectangle, and the sleeves, too, need only minimal shaping. For these you must decide on the number of stitches to be cast on at the wrist and the number of stitches required for the top of the sleeve, so that it will be large enough to go round the top of the arm. You can shape the sleeve gradually up the length of the sleeve until you have enough stitches to fit around the top arm, or do all the increasing needed on the last rib row at the wrist. The latter will give a full but attractive sleeve, and is obviously easier than graduated shaping, and this is the method that should be used for your first design.

**Measurement chart in centimetres**

| | | | | | | | |
|---|---|---|---|---|---|---|---|
| Bust | 81 | 86 | 91 | 97 | 102 | 107 | 112 |
| Sleeve seam | 42 | 43 | 43 | 43 | 43 | 44 | 44 |
| Wrist | 19 | 19 | 20 | 21 | 21 | 22 | 23 |
| Top arm (make larger for cardigans) | 29 | 30 | 32 | 33 | 34 | 36 | 37 |
| Armhole - jumper | 18 | 19 | 20 | 21 | 23 | 24 | 25 |
| Armhole - jacket | 19 | 20 | 21 | 23 | 24 | 25 | 27 |
| Raglan | 21 | 23 | 24 | 25 | 27 | 28 | 29 |
| Back neck | 14 | 14 | 15 | 15 | 17 | 17 | 18 |
| Neck drop | 5 | 5 | 5 | 6 | 6 | 6 | 6 |

**Measurement chart in inches**

| | | | | | | | |
|---|---|---|---|---|---|---|---|
| Bust | 32 | 34 | 36 | 38 | 40 | 42 | 44 |
| Sleeve seam | 16½ | 17 | 17 | 17 | 17 | 17½ | 17½ |
| Wrist | 7½ | 7½ | 7¾ | 8 | 8 | 8½ | 9 |
| Top arm | 11½ | 12 | 12½ | 13 | 13½ | 14 | 14½ |
| Armhole - jumper | 7 | 7½ | 8 | 8½ | 9 | 9½ | 10 |
| Armhole - jacket | 7½ | 8 | 8½ | 9 | 9½ | 10 | 10½ |
| Raglan | 8½ | 9 | 9½ | 10 | 10½ | 11 | 11½ |
| Back neck | 5½ | 5½ | 6 | 6 | 6½ | 6½ | 7 |
| Neck drop | 2 | 2 | 2 | 2½ | 2½ | 2½ | 2½ |

If you follow these guidelines and, where possible, check the dimensions given on the measurement chart with those of the person who will ultimately wear the garment, you should find designing your first sweater an exciting and rewarding project. Once you have tackled a drop-shoulder sweater you should have the confidence to go on to more complicated shapes. Once you understand how a pattern works, you will be able to use published patterns as guides and you can begin to experiment with different shaping by trying to adapt existing patterns to your own personal requirements.

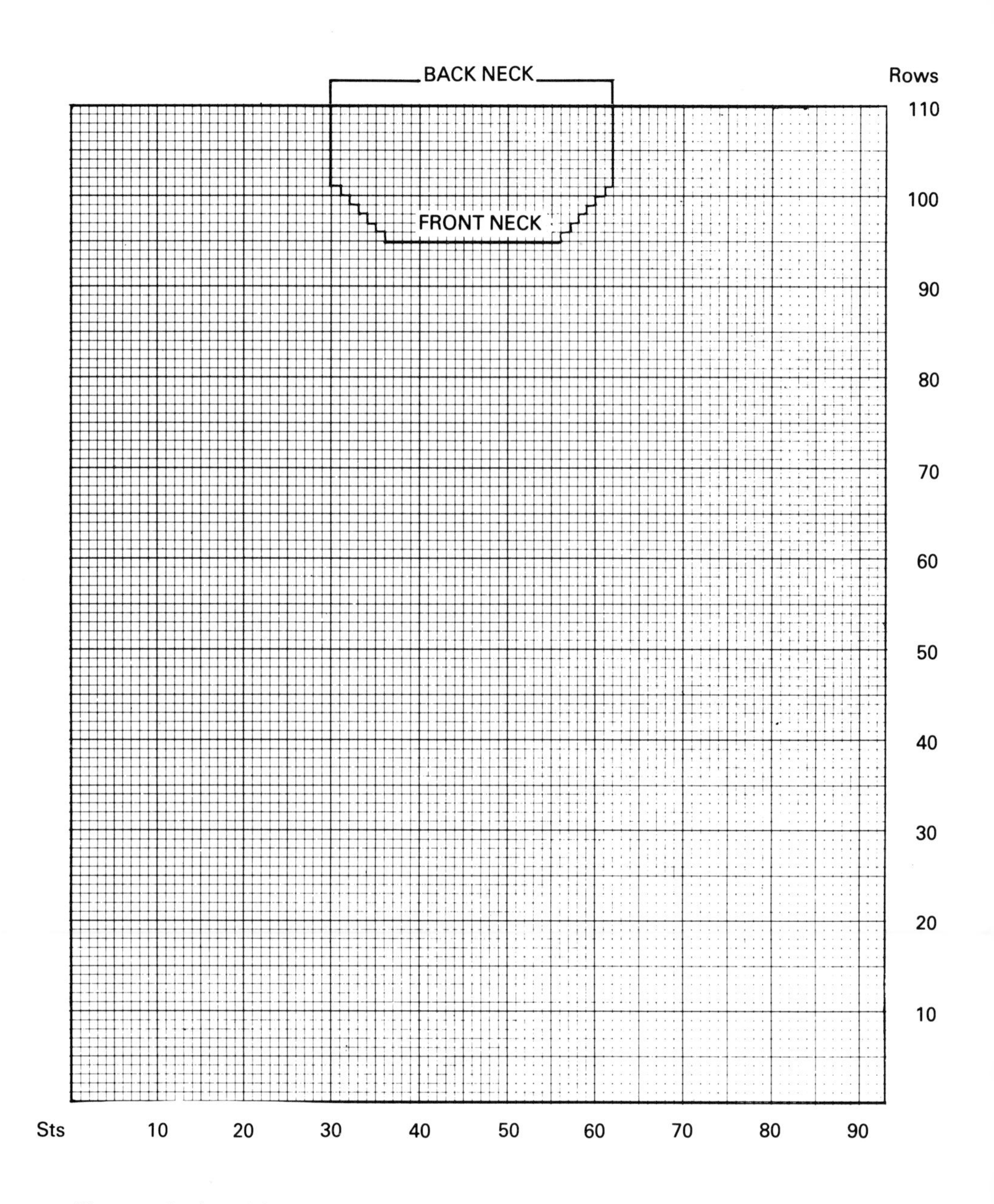


Chart 1 Back and front of drop-shoulder sweater. To fit an 86cm (34in) bust. Calculated for a tension of 20 sts and 22 rows to 10cm (4in).

# The knitting patterns

1

# STRIPED AND SIMPLE

A sweater in stocking stitch for the beginner

**Measurements**
To fit bust 81(86,91,96)cm (32[34,36,38]in)
Length 58cm (23in)
Sleeve seam 43cm (17in)

Striped and simple

## Materials

Of Emu Guernsey Pure New Wool, 6(7,8,9) 50g balls in main colour (Natural); 5(6,6,7) 50g balls in contrast colour (Scarlet).
1 pair each of 3¾ and 3mm knitting needles.

## Tension

13 sts and 17 rows to a 5 × 5cm square (2 × 2in) over st st on 3mm needles or size required to obtain correct tension.

## Front

Using 3¾mm needles and main colour, cast on 120(126,132,138) sts. Beg with a K row, work 9 rows st st. Change to 3mm needles. Work 2 rows K, then, beg with a K row, work 7 rows in st st. Next join in contrast colour and work 4 rows st st, then 4 rows st st in main colour. These 8 rows form the pattern.*
Cont in patt until work measures 51cm (20in) from hemline (garter stitch row), ending with a P row.
*Shape neck* as follows, at the same time keeping continuity of stripe patt.
*Next row:* K50(53,56,59) sts, turn, leaving rem 70(73,76,79) sts on spare needle. Working on these first 50(53,56,59) sts only, dec 1 st at neck edge on next and every foll row until 35(38,41,44) sts rem. Cont without shaping until work measures 58cm (23in), ending with a P row. Cast off.
Slip centre 20 sts on to length of yarn. Rejoin yarn to rem 50(53,56,59) sts. K1 row. Now work to match first side, reversing shapings.

## Back

Work exactly as given for front to *.
Cont in pattern until work measures 58cm (23in), ending with a P row. (This will form the last row of the back, so check that it is the same length as the front.)
*Next row:* cast off 35(38,41,44) sts, slip centre 50 sts on to length of yarn, cast off rem 35(38,41,44) sts.

## Sleeves

Using 3¾mm needles and main colour, cast on 52(56,60,64) sts. Beg with a K row, work 9 rows st st. Change to 3mm needles. Work 2 rows K, then, beg with a K row, work 7 rows in st st.
Joining in contrast colour, work in stripe patt, shaping sleeve

by inc 1 st at each end of next and every foll 7th row until there are 84(90,96,96) sts. Then work straight without shaping until work measures 43cm (17in) from hemline (garter stitch row). Cast off.

## Neckband and making up

Press all pieces according to pressing instructions on ballband. Join left shoulder seam. Using 3mm needles and main colour, and with right side facing, pick up and K 18 sts down right side neck, 20 sts from length of yarn at centre front neck, 18 sts up left side neck and 50 sts from length of yarn on back neck. Work 13 rows in K1 P1 rib on these 106 sts. Cast off loosely in rib.

Using a backstitch, sew up side seams, leaving 17(18,19,19)cm (6½[7,7½,7½]in) for the insertion of the sleeves. Join sleeve seams. Set in sleeves.
Using a slip stitch, sew up hems loosely on back, front and sleeves. Catch down ribbing at neck loosely on wrong side.

# 2

# RIBBONS

*(colour plate 1)*

A high-impact sweater that even the beginner can knit

**Measurements**
To fit bust 86(91,97)cm (34[36,38]in)
Length 51cm (20in)
Sleeve seam 43cm (17in)

**Materials**
Of Sunbeam Trophy Double Knitting, 4(5,6) 50g balls in main colour (A); 4(4,5) balls in each of 2 contrast shades.
1 pair each of 3¼, 4 and 5½mm knitting needles.

**Tension**
18½ (doubling up to 37 sts as per pattern) and 32 rows to 10cm (4in) over pattern on 4mm needles, or size required to obtain correct tension.

**Back**
Using 3¼mm needles and A cast on 83(89,95) sts.
*1st row:* K1, *P1, K1, rep from * to end.
*2nd row:* P1, *K1, P1, rep from * to end.
Rep these 2 rows for 5cm (2in) ending with a 2nd row.
Change to 4mm needles and work in patt as follows:
*1st–5th rows:* Using A, K.
Change to 5½mm needles and 1st contrast (B).
*6th row:* * K into back and front of next st; rep from * to end. 166(178,190) sts.
*7th–11th rows:* Beg with a P row, work in st st.
Change to 4mm needles and A.
*12th row:* *K2 tog; rep from * to end; 83(89,95) sts.
*13th–17th rows:* K.
Change to 5½mm needles and 2nd contrast (C).
*18th row:* As 6th row.

*19th–23rd rows:* As 7th–11th rows.
Change to 4mm needles and A.
*24th row:* As 12th row.
These 24 rows form patt.
Work 4 more patt repeats, ending on row 24.**
Using 4mm needles and A, cont in garter st for 10cm (4in).
*Shape shoulder*
*Next row:* Cast off 24(27,30) sts, K35, cast off rem 24 (27,30) sts.
Leave centre 35 sts on stitch holder.

## Front

Work as given for back to **.
Using 4mm needles and A, cont in garter st for 2cm (¾in), ending with right side facing.
*Shape neck*
*Next row:* K34(37,40), turn and leave rem sts on a spare needle. Dec 1 st at neck edge on every foll row to 24(27,30) sts, then cont until work measures same as back to shoulders. Cast off.
Return to the sts on spare needle; with wrong side facing slip centre 15 sts on to stitch holder; K to end.
Cont to match first side, reversing shaping.

## Sleeves

Using 3¼mm needles and A, cast on 35(37,41) sts and work in rib as on back for 4cm (1½in), ending with a 2nd row.
Change to 4mm needles and work in patt as given for back, inc 1 st at each end of next and every foll 6th row to 63(65,69) sts. Now cont in patt without shaping until 5 patt repeats have been completed, ending on row 24.
K 3 rows in A.
Cast off loosely.

## Neckband

Join right shoulder seam.
Using 3¼mm needles and A and with right side facing, pick up and K 20 sts down left neck, K up 15 sts from stitch holder at centre neck, pick up and K 20 sts up right neck and K across 35 sts from stitch holder at back neck. 90 sts.
Work 6 rows in K1 P1 rib. Cast off loosely in rib.

## To make up

Read pressing instructions on ballband.
Join left shoulder seam and neckband.
Sew in sleeves. Join side and sleeve seams.

3

# PINK AND PLAIN

For the beginner, in thick pure wool

**Measurements**
To fit bust 86(91,97)cm (34[36,38]in)
Length 54cm (21in)
Sleeve seam 43cm (17in)

**Materials**
Of Hayfield Gaucho, 8(9,10) 50g balls.
1 pair each of $5\frac{1}{2}$ and $6\frac{1}{2}$mm knitting needles.

Pink and plain

## Tension

8 sts and 11 rows to 10cm (4in) over pattern on 6½mm needles, or size required to obtain correct tension.

## Back

Using 5½mm needles cast on 45(47,49) sts.
*1st row:* K1, *P1, K1, rep from * to end.
*2nd row:* P1, *K1, P1, rep from * to end.
Rep these 2 rows for 5cm (2in), ending with a 2nd row and dec 5 sts evenly across last row. 40(42,44) sts.
Change to 6½mm needles and work in patt as follows:
*1st row:* (right side) P to end, winding yarn twice round needle for each st.
*2nd row:* K to end, winding yarn twice round needle for each st and dropping the extra loops from previous row.
*3rd row:* As 1st row, dropping the extra loops from previous row.
Rep the last 2 rows until work measures 34(33,32)cm (13½[13,12½]in) from beg, ending with a 2nd row.
*Shape armholes*
Cast off 2 sts at beg of next 2 rows, then dec 1 st at each end of next 3 rows. 30(32,34) sts. **
Cont without shaping until work measures 54cm (21in) from beg, ending with a 2nd row.
*Shape shoulders*
*Next row:* Cast off 7(8,9) sts, patt 16, including st on needle after casting off, cast off rem 7(8,9) sts.
Leave centre sts on a holder.

## Front

Work as given for back to **, then work 8 more rows.
*Shape neck*
*Next row:* Patt 12(13,14), turn and leave rem sts on a spare needle.
Dec 1 st at neck edge on next 5 rows, then cont until work measures the same as back to shoulders.
Cast off rem 7(8,9) sts.
Return to the sts on spare needle; with wrong side facing rejoin yarn and cast off 6 sts, patt to end.
Cont to match first side, reversing shaping.

## Sleeves

Using 5½mm needles cast on 25 sts, work in rib as on back for 5cm (2in), ending with a 2nd row and dec 5 sts evenly in last row. 20 sts.

Change to 6½mm needles and cont in patt as on back, inc 1 st at each end of every 5th row until there are 26(28,30) sts, then cont without shaping until sleeve, when slightly stretched, measures 43cm (17in) from beg, ending with a wrong side row.
*Shape top*
Cast off 2 sts at beg of next 2 rows.
Dec one st at each end of next and foll 1(2,3) alt rows, then at each end of every row until 8(10,12) sts rem. Cast off.

## Neckband

Join right shoulder seam.
Using 5½mm needles and with right side facing pick up and K 38 sts round front neck, then K back neck sts from holder. Work 4 rows in garter st, then cast off *loosely* knitwise.

## To make up

Do not press.
Join left shoulder seam and neckband.
Sew in sleeves. Join side and sleeve seams.

# 4

# CALYPSO

A multi-coloured all-wool sweater to brighten up those winter days

**Measurements**
To fit bust 76–81(86–91)cm (30–32[34–36]in)
Length 56cm (22in)
Sleeve seam 42(43)cm (16½[17]in)

Calypso

## Materials

Of Pingouin 4 Pingouin Double Knitting wool, 5(6) 50g balls in main colour (A); 2 balls in each of 5 contrast shades.
1 pair each of 3 and 3¾mm knitting needles.

## Tension

24 sts and 34½ rows to 10cm (4in) over pattern on 3¾mm needles or size required to obtain correct tension.
*Note:* The back and front of this sweater are knitted sideways.

## Back

Using 3¾mm needles and A, cast on 120 sts.
Joining in contrast shades as required, work in patt from chart, reading all odd rows K from right to left and even rows P from left to right, except for the rows to be worked in reverse stocking stitch as indicated in chart. **
Continue working from chart until 151(168) rows have been worked. Cast off.

## Front

Work as given for back to **.
Continue working from chart until 48(56) rows have been completed.
*Shape neck*
*Next row:* Cast off 4 sts, patt to end.
Keeping continuity of pattern as given on chart, dec 1 st at neck edge on next and every foll row to 102 sts. Work 25(26) rows, then inc 1 st at neck edge on next and every foll row to 116 sts. Cast on 4 sts at neck edge on foll row.
Cont in patt as given on chart without further shaping until all 151(168) rows have been completed to match back. Cast off.

## Sleeves

Using 3mm needles and A, cast on 38(42) sts. Work in K1 P1 rib for 6(7½)cm (2½[3]in), inc by 37(41) sts across rib row, evenly, to 75(83) sts.
Change to 3¾mm needles and joining in contrast shades as required, work in patt from chart for 117 rows. Cast off.

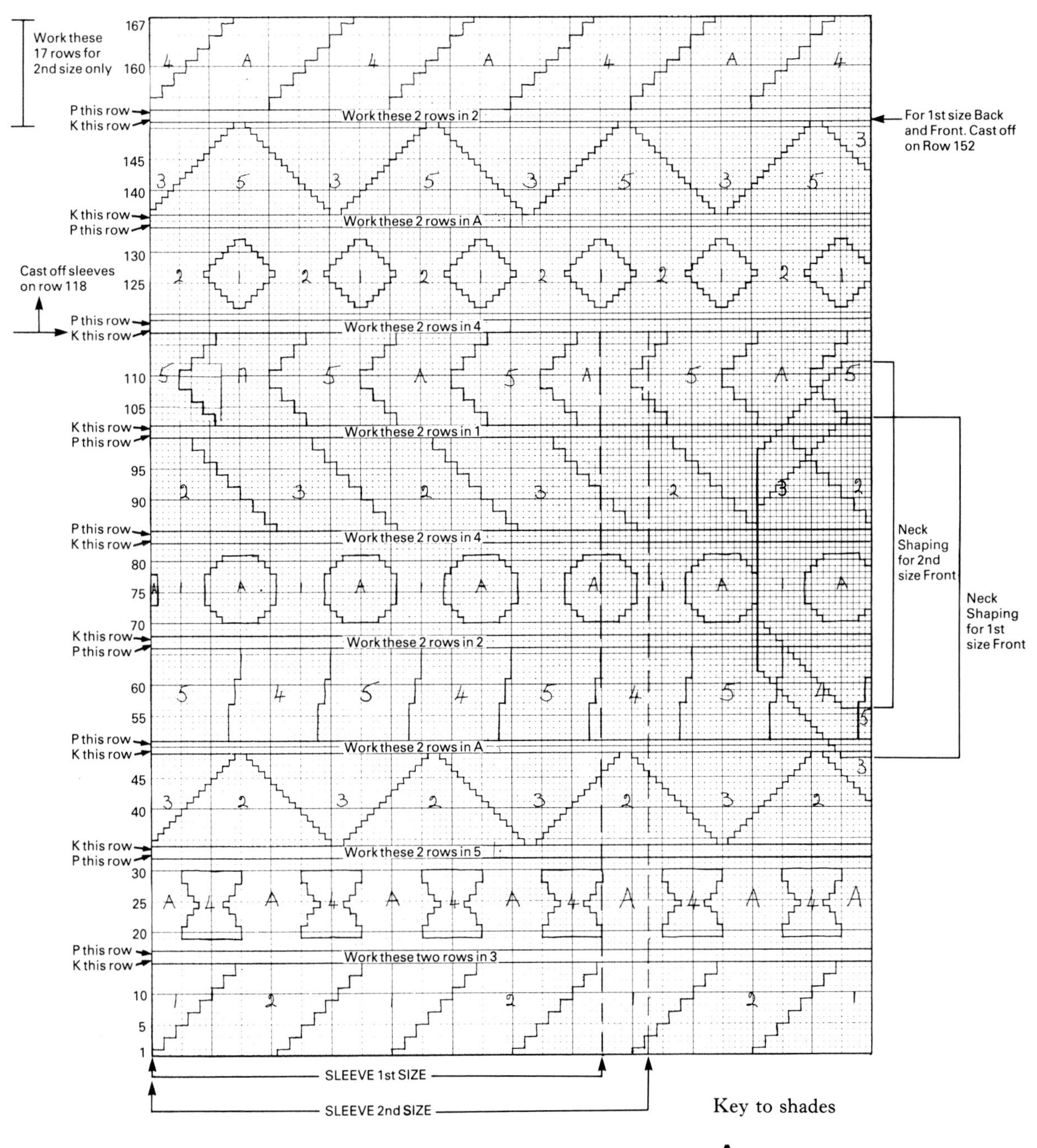


Key to shades

| | |
|---|---|
| A | Vanille (cream) |
| 1 | Kyoto (pink) |
| 2 | Pépite (yellow) |
| 3 | Vert D'eau (turquoise) |
| 4 | Azur (blue) |
| 5 | Corrida (scarlet) |

## Welts

Using 3mm needles and A, pick up and K 110(118) sts across bottom edge of front. Work 5cm (2in) K1 P1 rib. Cast off loosely in rib.

Work back welt to match.

## Neckband

Join right shoulder seam.
Using 3mm needles and A, and with right side facing, pick up and K 55(58) sts round front neck, then 40(44) sts from back neck between rows 49(57) and 104(113) of patt. Work 13 rows in K1 P1 rib. Cast off loosely in rib.

## To make up

Read pressing instructions on ballband.
Join left shoulder and neck band seam. Catch down neckband loosely on wrong side. Set in sleeves. Join side and sleeve seams.

# 5
# CABLED STRIPES
(*colour plate 2*)

A long, lean cabled sweater

## Measurements
To fit bust 81(86,91)cm (32[34,36]in)
Length 58(59, 60)cm (22½[23,23½]in)
Sleeve seam 43cm (17in)

## Materials
Of Sunbeam Pure New Wool Double Knitting, 8(9,10) 50g balls in main colour, Palm (M), 2(3,3) balls in each of 4 contrast colours, Banana (A), Lilac Dusk (B), Ice Blue (C) and Pale Green (D).
1 pair each of 3¼ and 4mm knitting needles.
Set of four 4mm needles; cable needle.

## Tension
26 sts and 36 rows to 10cm (4in) over pattern on 4mm needles, or size required to obtain correct tension.

## Back
Using 3¼mm needles and A cast on 97(109,109) sts.
*1st row:* K1, *P1, K1, rep from * to end.
*2nd row:* P1, *K1, P1, rep from * to end.
Rep these 2 rows once more.
Break off A, join in M and K 1 row, then cont in rib until work measures 7cm (3in) from beg, ending with a 1st row.
*Next row:* P to end, inc 13 sts evenly across last row, 110(122,122) sts.
Change to 4mm needles and work in patt as follows:
*1st row:* (right side) Using M, P4, (K6, P6) to last sts, K6, P4.
*2nd row:* Using M, K4 (P6, K6) to last 10 sts, P6, K4.
*3rd row:* As 1st row.
*4th row:* Using B, P to end.

*5th and 6th rows:* Using B, as 1st and 2nd rows.
*7th row:* Using B, P4 (sl next 3 sts on to cable needle to back of work, K3, then K3 from cable needle [called C6], P6) to last 10 sts, C6, P4.
*8th row:* Using M, P to end.
*9th row:* Using M, as 2nd row.
*10th row:* Using M, as 1st row.
*11th row:* As 9th row.
*12th row:* Using C, P to end.
*13th and 14th rows:* Using C, as 9th and 10th rows.
*15th row:* Using C, K4 (P6, C6) to last 10 sts, P6, K4.
*16th row:* Using M, P to end.
*17th–19th rows:* As 1st to 3rd rows.
*20th row:* Using D, P to end.
*21st–23rd rows:* Using D, as 5th to 7th rows.
*24th row:* Using M, P to end.
*25th–27th rows:* As 9th to 11th rows.
*28th row:* Using A, P to end.
*29th–31st rows:* Using A, as 13th to 15th rows.
*32nd row:* Using M, P to end.
These 32 rows form the patt; rep them twice more, then the first 20 rows again.
*Shape armholes*
Keeping patt correct, cast off 3(6,3) sts at beg of next 2 rows, then dec 1 st at each end of next 6 rows. 92(98,104) sts.**
Work 60(64,68) rows.
*Shape shoulders*
*Next row:* Cast off 28(31,34), patt 36, cast off rem 28(31,34) sts.
Leave the centre sts on a holder.

## Front

Cast on 109(109,121) sts and work as given for back as far as armholes.
*Shape armholes*
Keeping patt correct, cast off 9(6,9) sts at beg of next 2 rows, then dec 1 st at each end of next 6 rows. 92(98,104) sts.
Work 44(48,52) rows.
*Shape neck*
*Next row:* Patt 37(40,43), turn and leave rem sts on a spare needle. Dec 1 st at neck edge on next 9 rows, then cont without shaping until armhole measures the same as on back, ending with a wrong side row. Cast off.
Return to the sts on spare needle; with right side facing sl first 18 sts on to a holder, rejoin yarn and patt to end. Cont to match first side.

## Sleeves

Using 3¼mm needles and A cast on 47 sts and work 4 rows in rib as on back. Break off A, join in M, K 1 row, then cont in rib until work measures 6cm (2½in) from beg, ending with a 1st row.

*Next row:* P to end, inc 3 sts evenly across the row. 50 sts.

Change to 4mm needles and, beg with 17th patt row, cont in patt as on back, inc 1 st at each end of 5th and every foll 6th row, working the extra sts into patt, until there are 78(82,86) sts. Cont without shaping until 132 rows have been worked in patt, thus ending with the same patt row as at armholes on back and front.

*Shape top*

Keeping patt correct, cast off 7 sts at beg of next 2 rows.

Dec 1 st at each end of next and foll 2 alt rows, ending with a wrong side row.

Dec 1 st at each end of next and every 4th row until 44(48,52) sts rem, then work 3 rows.

Dec 1 st at each end of next and foll 5(6,7) alt rows, then at each end of foll 8 rows.

Cast off rem 16(18,20) sts.

## Polo collar

Join shoulder seams. Using set of four 4mm needles and M, and with right side facing, pick up and K 18 sts down left front neck, K front neck sts, pick up and K 18 sts up right front neck, then K back neck sts. 90 sts.

*Next row:* K to end, inc 20 sts evenly in the round.

Cont in rounds of K1, P1 rib for 24cm (9½in).

Break off M, join in A, P 1 round, then work 4 rounds in rib.

Cast off loosely in rib.

## To make up

Join side and sleeve seam. Sew in sleeves, noting that on 1st and 3rd sizes the side seams will come slightly to the back of the sleeve seams.

Press seams carefully according to instructions on ballband, taking care not to flatten the pattern.

6

# TRIANGLES

A jacket in two colours and two yarns, easy to knit and on big needles

## Measurements

To fit bust 81(86,91)cm (32[34,36]in)
Length 60cm (23½in)
Sleeve seam 44cm (17½in)

## Materials

Of Argyll Ambridge DK yarn, 8(9,10) 50g balls in main colour (Cobalt Blue); of Argyll Finesse Mohair, 9(10,11) 25g balls in contrast shade (Pompadour).
1 pair of 5½mm knitting needles.

## Tension

20 sts and 34 rows to 10cm (4in) over pattern on 5½mm needles, or size required to obtain correct tension.

*Note:* Use DK yarn double *throughout*.

## Back

Using 5½mm needles and 2 strands of main colour, cast on 88(94,102) sts. Work 8 rows K. Join in contrast shade and work in patt as follows:
*1st row:* (right side) K with main colour.
*2nd row:* With main colour, K7(6,6), wf, sl 2 pw, wb, *K6, wf, sl 2 pw, wb, rep from * to last 7(6,6) sts, K to end.
*3rd row:* With main colour, K7(6,6), sl 2 pw, *K6, sl 2 pw, rep from * to last 7(6,6) sts, K to end.
*4th row:* As 2nd row.
*5th row:* With contrast, K7(6,6), sl 2 pw, *K6, sl 2 pw, rep from * to last 7(6,6) sts, K to end.
*6th row:* With contrast, P7(6,6), sl 2 pw, *P6, sl 2 pw, rep from * to last 7(6,6) sts, P to end.

Triangles (*opposite*)

*7th–8th rows:* As 5th and 6th rows.
*9th row:* K with main colour.
*10th row:* With main colour, K3(2,2), wf, sl 2 pw, wb, *K6, wf, sl 2 pw, wb, rep from * to last 3(2,2) sts, K to end.
*11th row:* With main colour, K3(2,2), sl 2 pw, *K6, sl 2 pw, rep from * to last 3(2,2) sts, K to end.
*12th row:* As 10th row.
*13th row:* With contrast, K3(2,2), sl 2 pw, *K6, sl 2 pw, rep from * to last 3(2,2) sts, K to end.
*14th row:* With contrast, P3(2,2), sl 2 pw, * P6, sl 2 pw, rep from * to last 3(2,2) sts, P to end.
*15th–16th rows:* As 13th and 14th rows.
These 16 rows form pattern. Work 7 more pattern repeats, ending on a 16th row.
*Shape armholes*
Cast off 4 sts at beg of next 2 rows, then dec one st at each end of every row to 64(70,78) sts. Cont without shaping until 4 pattern repeats have been worked *from beginning of armhole shaping*, ending on a 16th row.
*Shape shoulders*
Cast off 16(19,23) sts at beg of next row, slip centre 32 sts on to stitch holder, cast off rem 16(19,23) sts.

## Left front

Using 5½mm needles and 2 strands of main colour, cast on 40(46,48) sts. Work 8 rows K. Join in contrast shade and work in patt as given for 1st (2nd, 1st) size for back until 8 pattern repeats have been completed, ending on a 16th row.
*Shape armhole*
Cast off 4 sts at beg of next row. Patt one row, then dec 1 st at armhole edge of every row to 28(34,36) sts.
Cont in patt without shaping for a further 22 rows.
*Shape neck*
*Next row:* Patt 20(26,28), turn, leaving rem 8 sts on safety pin. Dec 1 st at neck edge on every foll row to 16(19,23) sts, then cont in patt without shaping until work measures the same as back to shoulders.Cast off rem 16(19,23) sts.

## Right front

Work exactly as given for left front, but reversing shapings.

## Sleeves

Using 5½mm needles and 2 strands of main colour, cast on 64(70,70) sts. Work 8 rows K. Join in contrast shade and work in patt as given for 1st(2nd,2nd) size for back until 7 pattern repeats have been completed, then work 1st–8th rows of patt.

*Shape top*
Cast off 4 sts at beg of next 2 rows, then dec 1 st at each end of foll row. Next dec 1 st at each end of every 3rd row to 14(20,20) sts, then at each end of every alt row to 6(12,12) sts. Cast off.

## Front bands

Using 5½mm needles and 2 strands of main colour, cast on 10 sts. Work in garter st until band when slightly stretched fits up centre front. Leave on stitch holder. Make second band to match.

## Neckband and making up

Join shoulder seams. Sew on front bands.
Using 5½mm needles and 2 strands of main colour, and with right side facing, K up 10 sts from right band, 8 sts from right centre front; pick up and K 18 sts up right neck edge, K up 32 sts from back neck, pick up and K 18 sts down left neck edge, K up 8 sts from left centre front and 10 sts from left band. 104 sts.
K 4 rows.
*Next row:* K97, cast off 3 sts, K to end.
*Next row:* K4, cast on 3 sts, K to end.
K 2 more rows.
*Next row:* K9, K2 tog, K6, K2 tog, K16, K2 tog, K30, K2 tog, K16, K2 tog, K6, K2 tog, K9.
Cast off knitwise.
Sew in sleeves. Join side and sleeve seams.

## Button

Using 5½mm needles and contrast yarn, cast on 7 sts. Work 9 rows in reverse st st (right side P). Cast off.
Make second rectangle in exactly the same way.
Join 3 sides of the rectangle, insert a small amount of yarn as stuffing and sew up last side.
Sew button on to neck of jacket.

# 7

# IMPRESSIONIST

(*colour plate 3*)

A softly coloured Fair Isle sweater in a mohair-rich yarn

### Measurements

To fit bust 86(91,97)cm (34[36,38]in)
Length 56cm (22in)
Sleeve seam to fit 43cm (17in)

### Materials

Of Sunbeam Trophy Double Knitting, 1(2,2) 50g balls in Stone. Of Sunbeam Mohair, 3(3,4) 50g balls in each of Sage, Cerise, Primrose, Lilac, Mint and Saxe.
1 pair each of $4\frac{1}{2}$ and $5\frac{1}{2}$mm needles.

### Tension

21 sts and 20 rows to 10cm (4in) over pattern on $5\frac{1}{2}$mm needles, or size required to obtain correct tension.

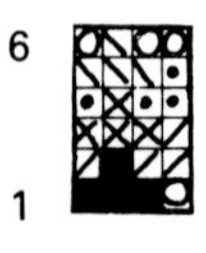


Key

Mint

Lilac

Saxe

Primrose

Cerise

Sage

### Back

Using $4\frac{1}{2}$mm needles and DK yarn, cast on 82(90,98) sts.
Work in K1 P1 rib for 8cm (3in), increasing evenly by 10 sts across last rib row. 92(100,108) sts.
Change to $5\frac{1}{2}$mm needles and mohair yarns and work in patt from chart, reading odd rows K from right to left and even rows P from left to right, and repeating the 4 patt sts 23(25,27) times across.
Cont until the 6 patt rows have been worked 9 times, ending on last patt row.
*Shape armholes*, keeping continuity of patt.
Cast off 5 sts at beg of next 2 rows, then dec 1 st at each end of next 8 rows to 66(74,82) sts. **
Cont in patt without shaping for a further 30 rows.

*Shape shoulders*
*Next row:* Cast off 16(18,20) sts, slip centre 34(38,42) sts on to length of yarn, cast off rem 16(18,20) sts.

## Front

Work as given for back to **, then work 14 rows.
*Shape neck*
*Next row:* Patt 23(25,27), turn and leave rem sts on a spare needle. Dec 1 st at neck edge on next 7 rows to 16(18,20) sts, then cont until work measures the same as back to shoulders. Cast off.
Return to the sts on spare needle; slip centre 20(24,28) sts on to a holder, rejoin yarn to rem sts and cont to match first side, reversing shapings.

## Sleeves

Using 4½mm needles and DK yarn cast on 44(48,52) sts.
Work in K1 P1 rib for 5cm (2in).
Change to 5½mm needles and mohair yarns and work in patt, reading chart as for back, until the 6 patt rows have been repeated 13 times, at the same time increasing by 1 st at each end of every 5th row to 64(68,72) sts.
*Shape top*
Keeping continuity of patt, cast off 6 sts at beg of next 2 rows. Dec one st at each end of next 2 rows, then at each end of every 3rd row to 34(38,42) sts. Next dec 1 st at each end of every following alternate row to 26(30,34) sts, then at each end of every row to 18(22,26) sts. Cast off.

## Neckband

Join right shoulder seam.
Using 4½mm needles and DK yarn, and with right side facing, pick up and K 16 sts from left neck, K up 20(24,28) sts from holder at centre back; pick up and K 16 sts from right neck and K up 34(38,42) sts from back neck. 86(94,100) sts.
Work 15 rows in K1 P1 rib, then cast of *loosely* in rib.

## To make up

Do not press.
Join left shoulder seam and neckband. Catch neckband down loosely on wrong side. Sew in sleeves. Join side and sleeve seams.

# 8

# CAROUSEL

(*colour plate 4*)

Bright colours and an unusual stitch for a warm spring sweater

### Measurements

To fit bust 86–91cm (34–36in)
Length 56cm (22in)
Sleeve seam 43cm (17in)

### Materials

Of Pingouin Mohair 70, 5 50g balls in main colour (A), 3 balls each in 4 contrast shades.
1 pair each of 3¼ and 4mm knitting needles.

### Tension

24 sts and 33 rows to 10cm (4in) over pattern on 4mm needles, or size required to obtain tension.

### Back

Using 3¼mm needles and A, cast on 101 sts.
*1st row:* K1, *P1, K1, rep from * to end.
*2nd row:* P1, *K1, P1, rep from * to end.
Rep these 2 rows for 7cm (2¾in), ending with a 2nd row and inc by 12 sts evenly across last row to 113 sts.
Change to 4mm needles and, beg with a K row, work 2 rows in st st.
Join 1st contrast shade (B), and work in patt as follows:
*1st row:* Using B, *K1, M1, K2, M1, K6 (K2 tog, K1) 3 times, K2 tog, K6, M1, K2, M1; rep from * to last st, K1.
*2nd row:* Using B, K.
*3rd row:*Using B, P.
*4th row:* Using B, K.
*5th row:* Using B, P
*6th row:* Using B, as 1st row.

Change to A.
*7th row:* Using A, K.
*8th row:* Using A, P.
*9th row:* Using A, K.
*10th row:* Using A, P.
Change to 2nd contrast shade (C).
*11th–16th rows:* Using C, as 1st–6th rows.
Change to A.
*17th–20th rows:* Using A, as 7th–10th rows.
Change to 3rd contrast shade (D).
*21st–26th rows:* Using D, as 1st–6th rows.
Change to A.
*27th–30th rows:* Using A, as 7th–10th rows.
Change to 4th contrast shade (E).
*31st–36th rows:* Using E, as 1st–6th rows.
Change to A.
*37th–40th rows:* Using A, as 7th–10th rows.
These 40 rows form the pattern.
Rep 1st–40th rows once, then work 1st–18th rows.
*Shape armholes*, keeping continuity of patt.
Cast off 5 sts at beg of next 2 rows, then cast off 2 sts at beg of foll 2 rows. Next dec 1 st at each end of every row to 85 sts.** Now cont in patt without shaping for a further 51 rows.
*Shape shoulders*
Cast off 22 sts, slip centre 41 sts on to spare needle, cast off rem 22 sts.

## Front

Work as given for back to **.
Now cont without shaping for a further 29 rows.
*Shape neck*, keeping continuity of patt.
*Next row:* Patt 34, turn and leave rem sts on a spare needle.
Dec 1 st at neck edge on next 12 rows to 22 sts, then cont until work measures the same as back to shoulders.
Cast off rem 22 sts.
Return to the sts on spare needle; slip centre 17 sts on to length of yarn, rejoin yarn to rem 34 sts, patt to end. Cont to match first side, reversing shaping.

## Sleeves

Using 3¼mm needles and A cast on 43 sts. Work in rib as on back for 5cm (2in), inc evenly by 42 sts on last row to 85 sts.
Change to 4mm needles and, beg with a K row, work 2 rows in st st.

Now work in patt, beg with 31st row, until 108 rows of patt have been worked.
*Shape top*, keeping continuity of patt.
Cast off 6 sts at beg of next 2 rows. Dec 1 st at each end of next 4 rows, then at each end of every alt row to 15 sts. Dec 1 st at each end of every row to 5 sts. Cast off.

## Collar

Using a backstitch seam, join left shoulder seam.
Using 3¼mm needles and A, cast on 8 sts and, using same needles and with right side facing, K up 41 sts from spare needle at back neck. Pick up and K 20 sts from left side neck, K up 17 sts from length of yarn at neck front and pick up and K 20 sts from right side neck.
*Next row:* Using same needles, cast on 8 sts in A, then work in K1 P1 rib across the 106 collar sts.
Work 8 more rows in K1 P1 rib across all collar sts.
*Make buttonhole*
*Next row:* Rib 108 sts, K2 tog, wf, rib to end.
*Next row:* Rib across all sts.
Cont in rib until collar measures 26cm (10in), making 5 more buttonholes evenly spaced along front collar edge.
Cast off loosely in rib.

## Buttons

*First side*
Using 3¼mm needles and A cast on 5 sts. Work 6 rows st st. Cast off.
*Second side*
As first side.

Make 5 more buttons in the same way, but using contrast shades.

## To make up

Do not press. Join right shoulder seam. Catch down collar at neckband. Sew in sleeves. Join side and sleeve seam. Sew together 3 edges of each button, stuff each button with small amount of yarn and sew up fourth edge. Stitch buttons on to collar.

9

# SOFTLY STRIPED

A dolman-sleeved sweater knitted in one piece

**Measurements**
To fit bust 86–91cm (34–36in)
Length 49cm (19in)
Sleeve seam to fit 43cm (17in)

Softly striped

## Materials

Of Pingouin Laine et Mohair, 3 balls of main colour (Vert D'eau) and 2 balls each of 4 contrast shades (Abricot, Rose, Lupin and Soleil).
1 pair each of 4 and 3¾mm knitting needles.

## Tension

16½ sts and 24½ rows to 10cm (4in) over patt on size 4mm needles, or size required to obtain correct tension.

## Front and back

*Note:* This garment is knitted in one piece, beginning at front welt.
Using 4mm needles and main colour, cast on 100 sts. Work 5cm (2in) K1 P1 rib, dec by 20 sts evenly along last row to 80 sts.
Joining contrast shades as required, work in patt as follows:
*1st row:* Using 1st contrast, K.
*2nd row:* As 1st row.
*3rd row:* Using 2nd contrast, K wrapping yarn twice round needle on every st.
*4th row:* Using 2nd contrast, K dropping off extra loop from previous row.
These 4 rows form pattern. Cont in patt for 6 more rows using 3rd, 4th and main colours in rotation, and continuing to use all colours in the same order and in rotation throughout the garment.
*Shape sides*, keeping continuity of patt, by inc 1 st at each end of next and every foll row to 150 sts, then inc 1 st at each end of every alt row to 204 sts.
Cont in patt without shaping for 4cm (1½in), ending with right side facing.
*Shape neck*
*Next row:* Patt 95, turn, leaving rem sts on spare needle. Working on these first 95 sts only, dec 1 st at neck edge on next and every foll row to 85 sts, keeping continuity of patt throughout. Work 3 rows without shaping, then inc 1 st on every row at neck edge to 93 sts, then cast on 18 sts at neck edge. These sts will form the back neck edge.
Rejoin yarn to rem 109 sts. Cast off first 14 sts at neck edge, then patt to end across rem 95 sts. Now work second side to match first, reversing shapings.
Patt across all 204 sts, then cont straight in patt without shaping for 20 rows.
*Shape sides*, keeping continuity of patt, by dec 1 st at each

end of next and every foll alt row to 150 sts, then at each end of every row to 80 sts. Patt 10 rows without shaping. Break off all but main colour and work 5cm (2in) K1 P1 rib, inc along first rib row evenly by 20 sts. Cast off loosely in rib.

## Cuffs

Using 3¾mm needles and main colour, pick up and K 42 sts along cuff edge.
Work 5cm (2in) K1 P1 rib. Cast off.
Work second cuff to match.

## Neckband and making up

Join side and cuff seams.
Using 3¾mm needles and main colour, cast on 8 sts.
*1st row:* (right side) P.
*2nd row:* K.
These 2 rows form reverse st st pattern. Cont in patt until rouleau edge, when slightly stretched, fits round neck edge. Cast off.
Sew rouleau around neck edge, placing edge seam at centre back.

10

# LACY STRIPES

A sweater with a forties look

**Measurements**
To fit bust 81(86,91)cm (32[34,36]in)
Length 48cm (19in)
Sleeve seam 42(43,43)cm (16½[17,17]in)

**Materials**
Of St John's Superwash 4 ply Pure Wool, 6(6,7) 25g balls in main shade (A) and 5(5,6) balls in contrast shade (B).
1 pair each of 2¾ and 3¼mm knitting needles.

Lacy stripes

*Scarf*
Of St John's Superwash 4 ply Pure Wool, 2 25g balls in main shade.
1 pair of 3¾mm knitting needles.

## Tension

31 sts and 48 rows to a 10 × 10cm square (4 × 4in) over pattern on 3¼mm needles or size required to obtain tension.

## Pattern

*1st row:* (right side) With A, K.
*2nd row:* With A, K1, *P3, K3; rep from * to last 4 sts, P3, K1.
*3rd row:* With B, K1, *sl 3, K3; rep from * to last 4 sts, sl 3, K1.
*4th row:* With B, P2, *sl 1, P5; rep from * to last 3 sts, sl 1, P2.
*5th row:* With B, K.
*6th row:* With B, K4, *sl 3, K3; rep from * to last st, K1.
*7th row:* With A, K4, *sl 3, K3; rep from * to last st, K1.
*8th row:* With A, P5, *sl 1, P5; rep from * to end.

## Back

Using 2¾mm needles and A, cast on 121(127,133) sts.
*1st row:* *P1, K1, rep from * to end.
*2nd row:* *K1, P1, rep from * to end.
Rep these two rows until work measures 5cm (2in). Work one more row in rib, inc by 16 sts evenly along row. 137(143,149) sts.
Change to 3¼mm needles and work in patt until back measures 33(32,31)cm (13[12½,12]in) ending with right side facing.
*Shape armholes* by casting off 6 sts at beg of next 2 rows, then dec 3 sts at beg of next 4 rows. Now dec 1 st at each end of every row to 99(105,111) sts. ** Cont without shaping until work measures 48cm (19in), ending with right side facing.
*Shape neck* by casting off 26(28,30) sts at beg of next row. Slip foll 47(49,51) sts on to length of yarn, cast off rem 26(28,30) sts.

## Front

Work as given for back to **, then cont in patt without shaping until work measures 43cm (17in), ending with right side facing.

*Shape neck* as follows:
*Next row:* Patt 37(38,39) sts, turn, leaving rem sts on spare needle.
Cont on these 37(38,39) sts only, dec 1 st at neck edge to 26(28,30) sts, then cont without shaping until front matches back, ending with right side facing. Cast off.
Rejoin yarn to rem 62(67,72) sts. Cast off centre 25(29,33) sts, patt to end.
Work second side to match first, reversing shapings.

## Sleeves

Using $2\frac{3}{4}$mm needles and A, cast on 59 sts. Work in rib as given for back until work measures 5cm (2in).
Change to $3\frac{1}{4}$mm needles and work in patt, inc 1 st at each end of every 3rd row to 101(107,111) sts. Cont without shaping until work measures 42(43,43)cm ($16\frac{1}{2}$[17,17]in) from beg, ending with right side facing.
*Shape top* by casting off 8(9,10) sts at beg of next two rows and 3(4,5) sts at beg of foll two rows. Dec 1 st at each end of foll 3(4,4) rows, then dec 1 st at each end of every 3rd row 5 times, then at each end of every 4th row 7(8,8) times. Now dec 1 st at each end of every row to 31(35,39) sts. Cast off.

## Neckband and making up

Using a backstitch seam, join right shoulder seam.
Using $2\frac{3}{4}$mm knitting needles and A pick up and K 25 sts down right neck, 25(29,33) sts across centre front neck; 25 sts up left neck and K across 47(49,51) sts from length of yarn on back neck. 122(128,134) sts. Work 8 rows in K1 P1 rib. Cast off loosely in rib.
Read pressing instructions on ballband. Using a backstitch seam, join left shoulder seam, side and sleeve seam. Set in sleeves, gathering in any fullness at the top of the sleeve.

## Scarf

Using $3\frac{3}{4}$mm needles and A, cast on 40 sts. Work in garter st (every row K) for 18 rows.
Change to $3\frac{1}{4}$mm needles and work in patt as follows:
*1st row:* K1, *K1, winding wool twice round needle, rep from * to last st, K1.
*2nd row:* K1, *K1, dropping off extra loops from previous row, rep from * to last st, K1.
These 2 rows form the patt. Cont in patt until work measures 124cm ($48\frac{1}{2}$in). Change to $3\frac{3}{4}$mm needles and work in garter st for 18 rows. Cast off.

11

# SWEET AND SIMPLE

(*colour plate 5*)

A quick-to-make sweater in chunky wool

**Measurements**
To fit bust 86(91,96)cm (34[36,38]in)
Length 55½cm (22in)
Sleeve seam 43cm (17in)

**Materials**
Of Chunky Wool from St John's Wools (available from P.O. Box 55, 39 Well Street, Bradford, BD1 5NG), 12(12,13) 50g hanks.
1 pair each of 5mm and 6mm knitting needles.

**Tension**
14 sts and 18 rows to a 10 × 10cm square (4 × 4in) over reverse stocking stitch on 6mm needles or size required to obtain tension.

**Back**
Using 5mm needles, cast on 57(61,65) sts. Work in K1 P1 rib until work measures 5cm (2in).
*Next row:* Inc (by working into front and back of st) 8 times evenly across row. 65(69,73) sts.
Change to 6mm needles.
*Next row:* P (right side of work).
*Next row:* K.
These 2 rows form the reverse st st patt. Cont in patt until work measures 37(36,35½)cm (14½[14¼,14]in), ending with wrong side facing.
*Shape armholes*
Cast off 2 sts at beg of next 2 rows, then dec by 1 st at each end of every row 6 times. 49(53,57) sts.* Now cont in patt

without shaping until work measures 55½cm (22in), ending with right side facing.
*Shape shoulders*
Cast off 11(12,13) sts at beg of next row, slip centre 27(29,31) sts on to stitch holder, then cast off rem 11(12,13) sts.

## Front

Work exactly as given for back to *.
Now cont in patt until work measures 48cm (19in), ending with right side facing.
*Shape neck as follows.*
*Next row:* P20(21,22), turn, leaving rem 29(32,35) sts on spare needle.
Cont on first 20(21,22) sts only, shaping neck by dec 1 st on neck edge on next and every foll row to 11(12,13) sts. Then cont straight in patt until front matches back. Cast off.
Rejoin yarn to rem 29(32,35) sts. Cast off centre 9(10,13) sts, P to end.
Now work second side to match first, reversing shapings.

## Sleeves

Using 5mm needles, cast on 30(32,34) sts. Work in K1 P1 rib until work measures 5cm (2in).
Change to 6mm needles, and work in patt beg with a P row, shaping sleeve by inc by 1 st at each end of every 6th row to 48(50,52) sts. Then cont in patt without shaping until sleeve measures 43cm (17in) from beg, ending with wrong side facing.
*Shape top*
Cast off 2 sts at beg of next two rows, then dec 1 st at each end of every foll row 3 times. Work 2 rows straight, then dec 1 st at each end of next and every foll 3rd row 5(5,6) times, then at each end of every alt row 1(2,1) times. Dec 1 st at each end of every row to 12(14,16) sts. Cast off.

## Neckband and making up

Using a backstitch seam, join right shoulder seam.
Using 5mm needles and with right side facing, pick up and K 13 sts down left side of front, 9(10,13) sts across centre front neck and 13 sts up right side of front and K across 27(29,31) sts from stitch holder on back neck. Work 4 rows K. Cast off loosely in garter st.
Join left shoulder seam and side seams. Sew up sleeve seams. Set in sleeves.

12

# JACK-IN-THE-BOX

*(front cover illustration)*

For the confident knitter, but not as difficult as it looks; the jack-in-the-box is knitted separately and sewn on afterwards

**Measurements**
To fit bust 86–91cm (34–36in) loosely
Length 55cm (21½in)
Sleeve seam 43cm (17in)

**Materials**
Of Sunbeam Trophy Double Knitting, 7 × 50g balls in main colour (A), 4 balls in first contrast (B), 1 ball in each of 3 contrast shades and in Black and Camel.
1 pair each of 3¼ and 4mm knitting needles.
7 buttons; sequins.

**Tension**
24 sts and 25 rows to 10cm (4in) over spot pattern on 4mm needles or size required to obtain correct tension.

**Back**
Using 3¼mm needles and A, cast on 95 sts. Work 5cm (2in) K1 P1 rib, inc evenly by 25 sts on last row to 120 sts.
Change to 4mm needles and K 1 row, then work in patt from chart, reading odd rows P from left to right and even rows K from right to left, and shaping armholes on 80th row as indicated on chart.
When armhole shaping has been completed, cont straight without any further shaping until all 135 rows of patt have been completed.
*Shape neck*
*Next row:* Cast off 27 sts, K36 in 3, cast off remaining 27 sts.

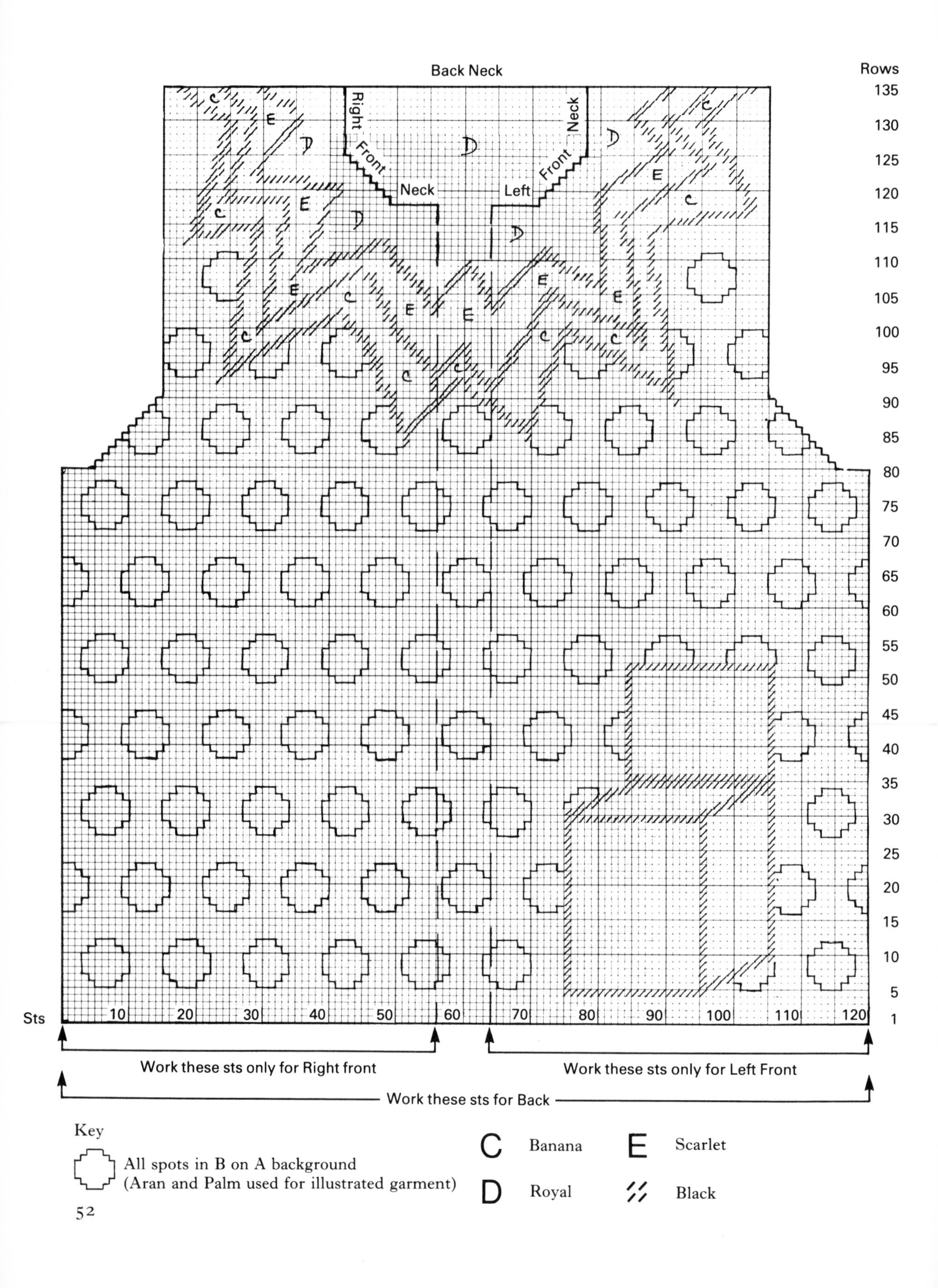

Back Neck
Rows
135
130
125
120
115
110
105
100
95
90
85
80
75
70
65
60
55
50
45
40
35
30
25
20
15
10
5
1
Right Front Neck
Left Front Neck
C
D
E
Sts
10
20
30
40
50
60
70
80
90
100
110
120
Work these sts only for Right front
Work these sts only for Left Front
Work these sts for Back
Key
All spots in B on A background
(Aran and Palm used for illustrated garment)
C Banana
D Royal
E Scarlet
// Black

Rejoin yarn to centre 36 sts, P one row. Leave rem sts on stitch holder.

**Left front**

Using $3\frac{1}{4}$mm needles and A, cast on 44 sts. Work 5cm (2in) K1 P1 rib, inc evenly by 12 sts on last row, to 56 sts.
Change to 4mm needles and K 1 row, then work in patt from chart for left front, reading rows as for back and shaping armholes and neck as indicated on chart, until all 135 rows of patt have been completed. Cast off.

**Right front**

Work exactly as given for left front, but working from chart for right front.

**Sleeves**

Using $3\frac{1}{4}$mm needles and A, cast on 42 sts. Work 2cm ($\frac{3}{4}$in) K1 P1 rib, working twice into every st on last row, thereby inc to 84 sts.
Change to 4mm needles and, beg with a P row, work 5 rows st st.
Joining in B, work in spot patt thus:
*1st row:* K1B, *9A, 3B; rep from * to last 11 sts, 9A, 2B.
*2nd row:* P3B, *7A, 5B; rep from * to last 9 sts, 7A, 2B.
*3rd row:* K3B, *5A, 7B; rep from * to last 9 sts, 5A, 4B.
*4th row:* P4B, *5A, 7B; rep from * to last 9 sts, 5A, 4B.
*5th row:* As 3rd row.
*6th row:* P3B, *7A, 5B; rep from * to last 9 sts, 7A, 2B.
*7th row:* As 1st row.
*8th row:* P in A.
*9th row:* K in A.
*10th row:* As 8th row.
*11th row:* As 9th row.
*12th row:* P5A, *3B, 9A; rep from * to last 7 sts, 3B, 4A.
*13th row:* K3A, *5B, 7A; rep from * to last 9 sts, 5B, 4A.
*14th row:* P3A, *7B, 5A; rep from * to last 9 sts, 7B, 2A.
*15th row:* K2A, *7B, 5A; rep from * to last 10 sts, 7B, 3A.
*16th row:* As 14th row.
*17th row:* As 13th row.
*18th row:* As 12th row.
*19th row:* K in A.
*20th row:* P in A.
*21st row:* As 19th row.
*22nd row:* As 20th row.

Repeat these rows 2 more times, then work 1st–20th rows.
*Shape top*, keeping continuity of spot patt.
Cast off 6 sts at beg of next 2 rows, then dec 1 st at each end of foll 5 rows. Work 2 rows without shaping, then dec 1 st at each end of next and every foll 4th row 6 times, then at each end of every foll 3rd row 5 times. Dec 1 st at each end of every alt row twice, then at each end of every row to 26 sts. Cast off.

## Button and buttonhole bands

Using 3¼mm needles and A, cast on 10 sts. Work in K1 P1 rib until band, when slightly stretched, fits up left front to neck. Leave sts on stitch holder.
Work buttonhole band to match, but making buttonhole thus on 4th row and then at every 8cm (3¼in) until 6 holes have been worked.
*Buttonhole row:* K1, P1, K1, P1, K2 tog, wf, K1, P1, K1, P1.
*Next row:* (K1, P1) to end.

When 6 buttonholes have been worked, cont in rib until right band matches left. Leave sts on stitch holder.

## Neckband

Join shoulder seams. Sew bands in place.
Using A, 3¼mm needles and with right side facing, K up 10 sts from right front band. Pick up and K 7 sts from right centre front; pick up and K 17 sts up right side front. K across 36 sts at back, then pick up and K 17 sts down left side front. Pick up and K 7 sts from left centre front and K across 10 sts on left band.
Work in K1 P1 rib for 6 rows, at the same time working buttonhole on right neck edge as before on 3rd row. Cast off loosely in rib.

## Pocket and jacks

### *Pocket*

Using 4mm needles and Black, cast on 21 sts, K 2 rows.
Join in contrast shade C, and work thus:
*1st row:* K1 Black, K19 C, K1 Black.
*2nd row:* P1 Black, P19 C, P1 Black.
*Note:* Use 2 small balls of Black; do not carry yarn right across work. Repeat these 2 rows 10 more times, then work 1st row once.

Break off C. Work 1 row K in Black. Cast off knitwise in Black.

*Jacks* (make 2)
*Hat:* Using 3¼mm needles and Black, cast on 16 sts. Beg with a K row, work 2 rows st st.
Cast off 3 sts at each end of next row, then work 3 rows st st on remaining 10 sts. Cast off.
*Face:* Using 3¼mm needles and Camel, cast on 4 sts. K 1 row. Inc 1 st at each end of next and every foll row to 12 sts. Work 3 rows st st without shaping. Cast off.
*Body:* Using 3¼mm needles and D, cast on 8 sts. Beg with a K row, work 6 rows st st. Change to E and work a further 12 rows st st. Cast off.
*Arms:* Using 3¼mm needles and D, cast on 22 sts. Beg with a K row, work 4 rows st st. Cast off. (Make 2 for each jack.)
*Hands:* Using 3¼mm needles and Camel, cast on 3 sts. Work 4 rows st st. Cast off.
*Bow-tie:* Using 3¼mm needles and C, cast on 15 sts. Beg with a K row work 8 rows st st. Cast off.

## To make up

Join side and sleeve seams. Set in sleeves, gathering sleeve at shoulder.
Sew on buttons. Sew pocket on to front using Black.
Stitch jacks on to front and back, placing a little yarn for stuffing behind each piece, and wrapping a length of C around middle of bow-tie before stitching it down.
Embroider face and buttons and hair on to jacks.
Stitch on sequins at random on hat and tie of jacks and around top of cardigan.

# 13

# SEASHORE

*(colour plate 6)*

Muted colours and intricate patterns to remind you of the summer – but only for the very experienced knitter

Key

- Clerical Grey
- Banana
- Silver Blue
- Pink Dawn
- Water Green
- French Rose
- Champagne
- Driftwood
- Ivory

### Measurements

To fit bust 91–97cm (36–38in)
Length 56cm (22in)
Sleeve seam to fit 43cm (17in)

### Materials

Of Sirdar Majestic Double Knitting wool, 3 50g balls in Banana; 2 balls in each of Water Green, Silver Blue and Ivory; 1 ball in each of French Rose, Pink Dawn, Clerical Grey, Champagne and Driftwood.
1 pair each of $3\frac{1}{4}$ and 4mm knitting needles.
6 pearl buttons/beads; packet of silver/pearl sequins.

### Tension

23 sts and 26 rows to 10cm (4in) over pattern on 4mm needles, or size required to obtain correct tension.

Chart 1

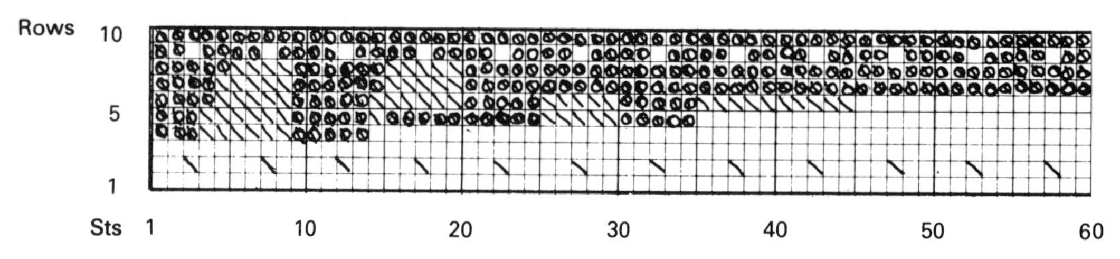


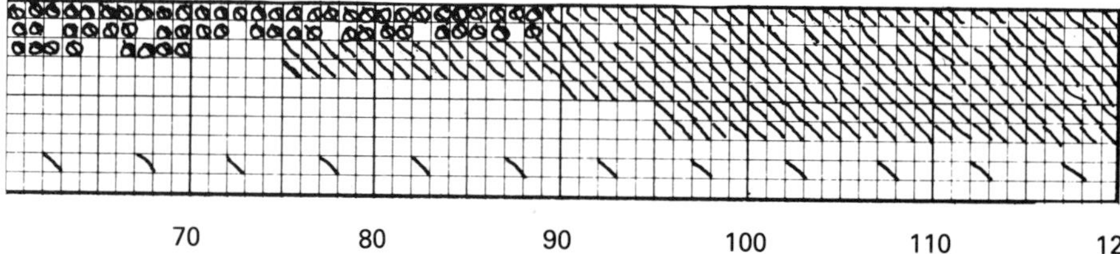

## Back

Using 3¼mm needles and Grey, cast on 90 sts. Work 4 rows K1 P1 rib.
Break off Grey yarn, join in Banana, K1 row then cont in rib until work measures 5cm (2in) from beginning, ending with right side facing, and inc evenly by 30 sts on last row to 120 sts. Change to 4mm needles and work in patt from Chart 1, reading odd rows K from right to left and even rows P from left to right and joining in contrast shades as required.
When all 10 rows of Chart 1 have been completed, cont in patt from Chart 2, reading odd and even rows as before and repeating the 20 patt sts 6 times across each row and repeating the 20 patt rows 3 times in all.
When 60 rows have been completed in patt from Chart 2, work in patt from Chart 3, reading chart as before and shaping armholes on 13th and 14th rows as indicated on chart. **When all armhole shaping has been completed, continue straight in pattern from chart without any further decreasing until all 70 rows of Chart 3 have been worked.

*Shape neck*

*71st row:* Using Banana, cast off 28 sts, K across centre 40 sts, cast off rem 28 sts.
Leave centre 40 sts on spare needle.

Chart 2

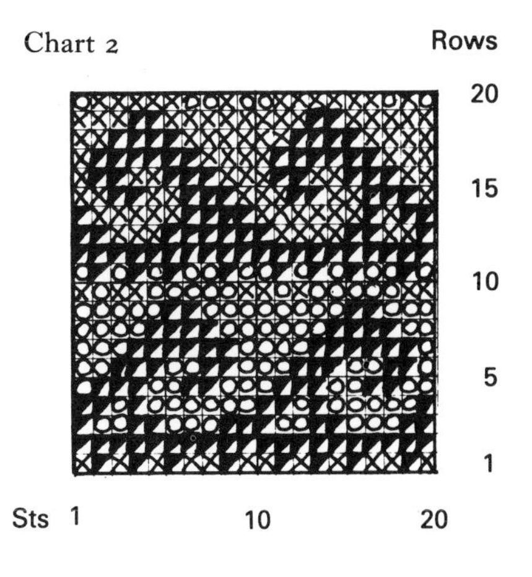


Chart 3

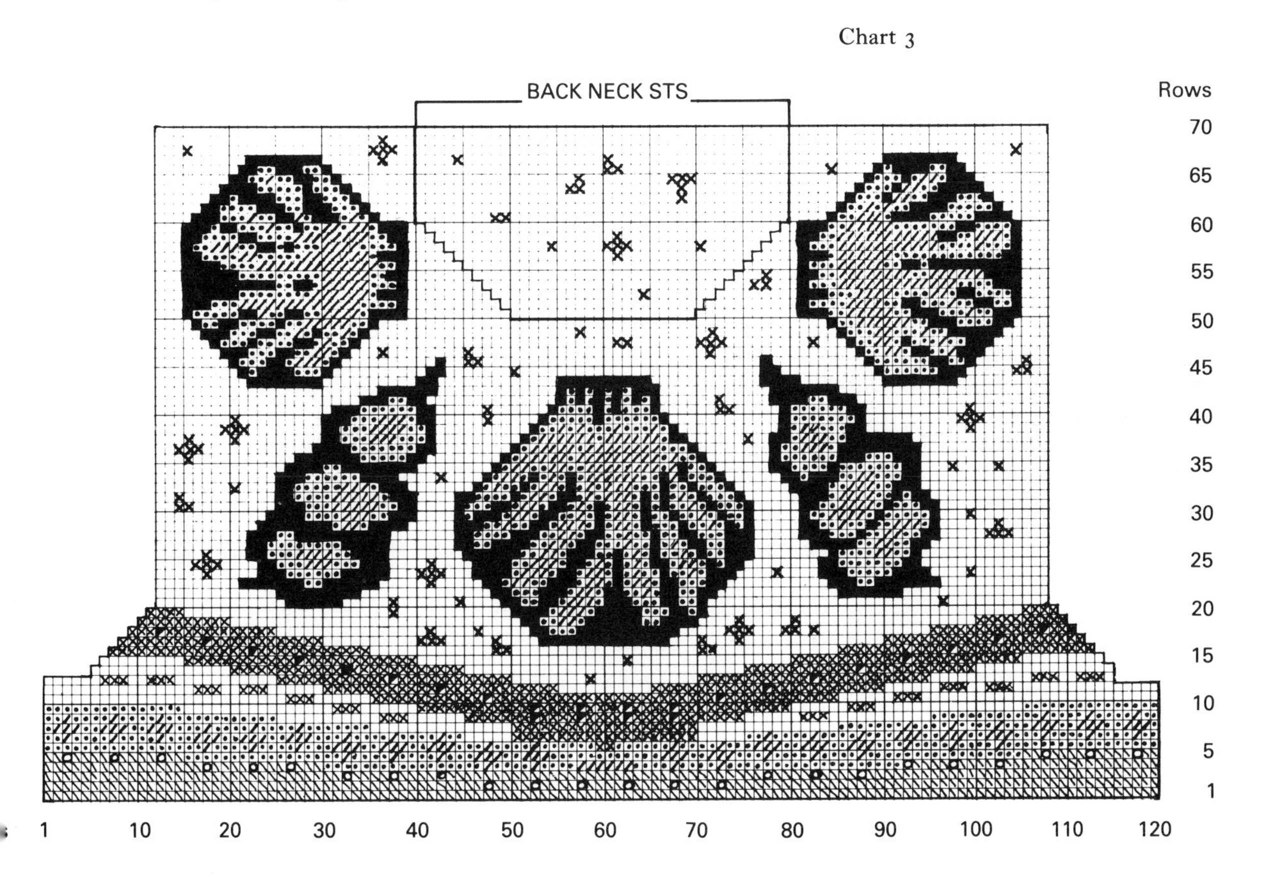

## Front

Work as given for back to **.
Cont working from chart to 50th row, completing armhole shaping as for back.

*Shape neck*

*51st row:* Patt 38, turn, leaving rem sts on spare needle.
Working on first 38 sts only, dec 1 st at neck edge on next and every foll row to 28 sts, keeping continuity of patt as indicated on chart throughout.
Work straight in patt until 70th row has been completed, then cast off.
Slip centre 20 sts on to length of yarn; rejoin yarn to rem 38 sts and patt to end.
Work to match first side, working patt as on chart, reversing shapings.

## Sleeves

Using 3¼mm needles and Clerical Grey, cast on 40 sts. Work 4 rows K1 P1 rib. Break off Grey yarn, join in Banana, K1 row and cont in rib until work measures 38mm (1½in) from beg, ending with right side facing and having worked twice into every st on last rib row to 80 sts.

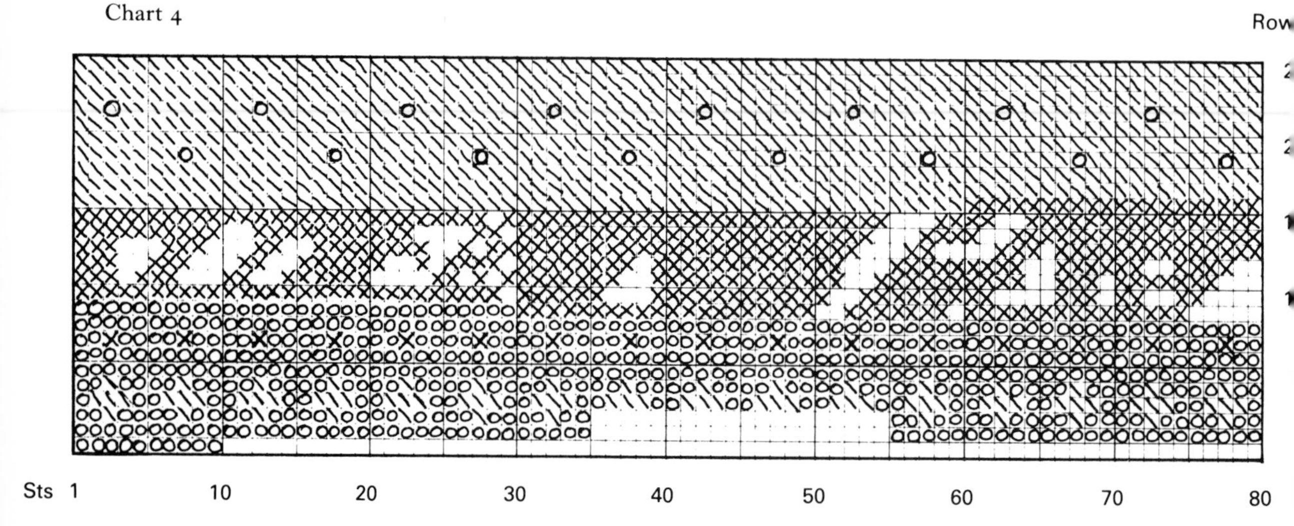


Change to 4mm needles and work in patt from Chart 4, reading as for Chart 1. When all 26 rows have been completed, cont in patt from Chart 2, repeating the 20 patt sts 4 times across and repeating the 20 patt rows 3 times in all.
When 60 rows have been completed in patt from Chart 2,

Chart 5

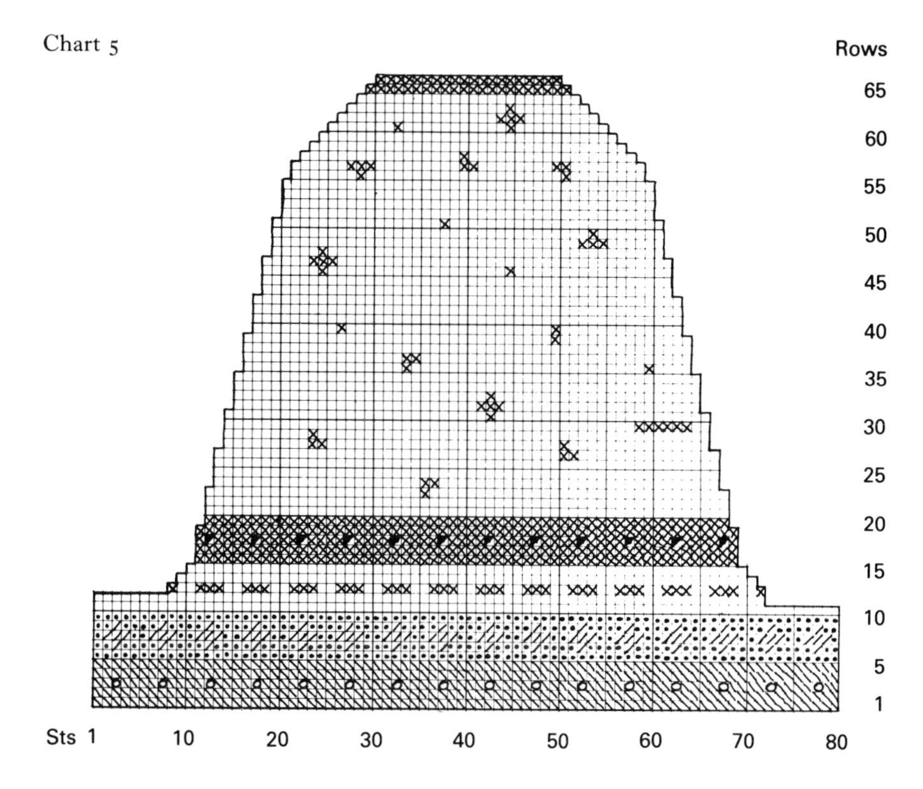


cont in patt from Chart 5, shaping top sleeve as indicated on chart. Cast off rem 20 sts.

## Neckband

Join right shoulder seam in Banana.
Using $3\frac{1}{4}$mm needles and Banana, and with right side facing, pick up and K 20 sts down left side front neck, K across 20 centre front sts, pick up and K 20 sts up right side front neck and K across 40 sts from back neck. Beg with a P row, work 6 rows st st; break off Banana yarn and join Clerical Grey.
Work 1 row st st.
*Next row:* *K2 tog., wf, rep from * to end.
*Next row:* P in Clerical Grey.
Break off grey yarn and rejoin Banana. Work a further 5 rows st st. Cast off loosely.

## To make up

Join left shoulder seam and neckband. Catch neckband down loosely on wrong side. Join side and sleeve seams. Set in sleeves, gathering any fullness at shoulder. Sew pearl buttons on to shells and scatter sequins around neck of sweater and sew on.

14

# FRUIT-DROP

*(colour plate 7)*

Quick and easy to knit, in pure cotton and bright summer colours

### Measurements

To fit bust 81–86 (91–97)cm (32–34[36–38]in)
Length 57cm (22½in)
Sleeve seam 43cm (17in)

### Materials

Of Pingouin Fil D'Ecosse No 3, 9(10) 50g balls in main colour (A); 4 balls in each of 2 contrast shades (B and C); 3 balls in third contrast shade (D).
1 pair each of 3¼ and 4mm knitting needles.

### Tension

22 sts and 36 rows to 10cm (4in) over pattern on 4mm needles, or size required to obtain correct tension.

### Back

Using 3¼mm needles and A, cast on 85(93) sts. Work in rib thus:
*1st row:* K1, *P1, K1; rep from * to end.
*2nd row:* P1, *K1, P1; rep from * to end.
Rep these 2 rows for 7½cm, ending with a 2nd row and inc evenly by 15 sts across last row to 100(108) sts.
Change to 4mm needles and work in patt thus:
*1st row:* K in A.
*2nd row:* P in A.
*3rd row:* *In D, K3, sl 1; rep from * to end.
*4th row:* *In D, sl 1, wf, K3, wb; rep from * to end.
*5th row:* K in A.
*6th row:* P in A.
*7th row:* In B, K1, *sl 1, K3; rep from * to last 3 sts, sl 1, K2.

*8th row:* In B, K2, *wb, sl 1, wf, K3; rep from * to last 2 sts, wb, sl 1, wf, K1.
*9th row:* As 7th row.
*10th row:* As 8th row.
*11th–20th rows:* As 1st–10th rows, but reading C for B.
These 20 rows form the pattern.
Rep these 20 patt rows 5 times, ending on 20th row.
*Shape armholes*
Cast off 5 sts at beg of next 2 rows, then dec 1 st at each end of every row to 72(80) sts.**
Cont straight in patt without further shaping until 70 rows have been worked from beginning of armhole shaping.
*Shape shoulders*
Cast off 10(12) sts at beg of next 2 rows, then 9(10) sts at beg of foll 2 rows. Leave rem 34(36) sts on spare needle.

**Front**
Work as given for back to **.
Cont straight in patt until work measures 49cm (19in) from beg, ending with right side facing.
*Shape neck*
*Next row:* Patt 27(30) sts, turn, leaving rem sts on spare needle.
Dec 1 st at neck edge on next and every foll row to 19(22) sts, then cont in patt until work matches back to shoulders, shaping shoulder as for back.
Return to the sts on the spare needle; with right side facing, rejoin yarn and cast off centre 18(20) sts; patt to end.
Cont on rem 27(30) sts to match first side, reversing shaping.

**Sleeves**
Using 3¼mm needles and A, cast on 44(48) sts. Work for 5cm (2in) in K1 P1 rib.
Change to 4mm needles and work in patt, beg with 15th row and inc 1 st at each end of next and every 6th row to 72 (76) sts.
Work in patt without shaping until 146 patt rows have been worked from beg of sleeve.
*Shape top*
Cast off 5 sts at beg of next 2 rows, then dec 1 at each end of every row to 58(62) sts. Next dec 1 st at each end of every 3rd row to 20, then at each end of every alt row to 10(12) sts.
Cast off.

## Neckband

Join right shoulder seam.
Using A and $3\frac{1}{4}$mm needles and with right side facing, pick up and K 21 sts down left side front, 18(20) sts from centre front, 21 sts up right side front and K up 34(36) sts from sts at back on spare needle. Work 6 rows K1 P1 rib, then cast off loosely in rib.

## To make up

Read and follow pressing instructions on ballband.
Join left shoulder seam and neckband.
Join side and sleeve seams. Sew in sleeves.

# 15
# CANDY STRIPES
(*colour plate 8*)

Easy to knit in cool crunchy cotton

**Measurements**
To fit bust 86(91,97)cm (34[36,38]in)
Length 56cm (22in)
Sleeve seam to fit 43cm (17in)

**Materials**
Of Pingouin Fil D'Ecosse No. 3 cotton, 5(6,6) 50g balls in main colour (A), 2(3,3) 50g balls in each of 3 contrasting colours.
1 pair each of 3¾ and 4mm knitting needles.

**Tension**
14 sts and 25 rows to 10cm (4in) over pattern on 4mm needles, or size required to obtain correct tension.

**Back**
Using 3¾mm needles and 1st contrast shade, cast on 85(87,91) sts.
*1st row:* K1, *P1, K1, rep from * to end.
*2nd row:* P1, *K1, P1, rep from * to end.
Rep these 2 rows once more. Change to A and K 1 row.
Now cont in rib as before in A until work measures 5cm (2in) from beg, ending with wrong side facing and dec 20(19,20) sts evenly across last row to 65(68,71) sts.
Change to 4mm needles and work in pattern as follows.
*1st row:* Using A, K (wrong side).
*2nd row:* Using A, K (right side).
*3rd row:* Using A, K1, *K1, winding yarn twice round needle for each st; rep from * to last st, K1.
*4th row:* Using A, K, dropping the extra loops from previous row.
*5th–8th rows:* Using 2nd contrast shade, as 1st–4th rows.
*9th–12th rows:* Using 1st contrast shade, as 1st–4th rows.
*13th–16th rows:* Using 3rd contrast shade, as 1st–4th rows.

These 16 rows form pattern.
Work these 16 pattern rows 6 more times, then work 1st–4th rows once.**
Break off all contrast shades and cont in garter st (every row knit) for 4cm (1½in) ending with right side facing.
*Shape shoulders*
Cast off 9 sts at beg of next 4 rows. Leave centre 29(32,35) sts on a holder.

## Front

Work as given for back to **, then break off all contrast shades and work 1 row K.
*Shape neck*
*Next row:* K25, turn and leave rem sts on a spare needle. Cont on these 25 sts only, working in garter st and dec 1 at neck edge on next 7 rows to 18 sts, then cont without shaping until work measures the same as back to shoulder shaping, ending with right side facing.
*Shape shoulders*
Cast off 9 sts at side edge on next row. K 1 row. Cast off rem 9 sts.
Return to the sts on spare needle. Slip centre 15(18,21) sts on to length of yarn; rejoin yarn to rem 25 sts, K to end. Work to match first side, reversing shapings.

## Sleeves

Using 3¾mm needles and 1st contrast, cast on 35(39,42) sts. Work in rib as on back for 5cm (2in), changing to A on 5th row as given for back, and ending with a 2nd row. Inc evenly by 26 sts in last row to 61(65,68) sts. Change to 4mm needles and cont in patt as on back, beg with 9th row, until 5½ pattern repeats have been worked. Break off all contrast shades and work 1½cm (⅝in) in garter st in A. Cast off.

## Neckband

Join right shoulder seam.
Using 4mm needles and A and with right side facing, pick up and K 14 sts down left side neck, and K up centre 15(18,21) sts from length of yarn. Pick up and K 14 sts up right side neck and K up 29(32,35) sts from back. 72(78,84) sts.
Work 4 rows in garter st. Cast off loosely knitwise.

## To make up

Do not press.
Join left shoulder and neckband. Using a backstitch seam, join side and sleeve seams. Set in sleeves.

16

# COTTON AND CREAM

Cotton and cream

## Measurements

To fit bust 86(91,97)cm (34[36,38]in)
Length 51cm (20in)
Sleeve seam 18cm (7in)

## Materials

Of Sunbeam Susanna cotton, 10(11,12) 50g balls.
1 pair each of $3\frac{1}{4}$ and 4mm knitting needles.

## Tension

27 sts and 36 rows to 10cm (4in) over pattern on 4mm needles, or size required to obtain correct tension.

## Back

Using $3\frac{1}{4}$mm needles cast on 100(110,120) sts. Work in K1 P1 rib for 5cm (2in), increasing evenly by 21 sts across last rib row. 121(131, 141) sts. Change to 4mm needles and work in patt as follows.
*1st row:* K (right side).
*2nd row:* K.
*3rd row:* P.
*4th row:* K.
*5th row:* *K1, (K2 tog) twice, (wrn, K1) 3 times, wrn, (K2 tog tbl) twice; rep from * to last st, K1.
*6th row:* P, working into back of every made st.
*7th–12th rows:* Rep 5th and 6th rows 3 times.
Rep these 12 patt rows 12 more times,** then work in garter st for 3cm ($1\frac{1}{4}$in), ending with right side of work facing.
*Shape neck*
*Next row:* K 29(34,39) sts, turn and leave rem sts on a spare needle. Working on these 29(34,39) sts only, dec 1 st at neck edge on next 2 rows to 27(32,37) sts; K 1 row without shaping and cast off in garter st.
Return to the sts on spare needle; slip centre 63 sts on to stitch holder, rejoin yarn to rem 29(34,39) sts, K to end. Cont to match first side, reversing shaping.

## Front

Work as given for back to **, then work 2 rows in garter st.
*Shape neck*
*Next row:* K38(43,48), turn and leave rem sts on a spare needle. Working every row K, dec 1 st at neck edge on next 11 rows to 27(32,37) sts, then cont until work measures the same as back to shoulders. Cast off knitwise.

Return to the sts on spare needle; slip centre 45 sts on to length of yarn, rejoin yarn to rem 38(43,48) sts, K to end. Work to match first side, reversing shaping.

## Sleeves

Using 4mm needles, cast on 91(101,101) sts. K 2 rows, then work in patt as given for back, repeating the 12 patt rows 5 times. K 2 rows. Cast off knitwise.

## Neckband

Join right shoulder seam.
Using 4mm needles and with right side facing, pick up and K 14 sts down left side neck. K 45 sts from length of yarn at neck front, pick up and K 14 sts up right side neck and K 63 sts from stitch holder at back neck.
Work 4 rows in garter st, then cast off loosely knitwise.

## To make up

Do not press.
Join left shoulder seam and neckband.
Sew in sleeves. Using a backstitch seam, join side and sleeve seams.

17

# BOLD AND BRIGHT

A Fair Isle jacket in clear, bright colours

**Measurements**
To fit bust 76–81(91–97)cm (30–32[36–38]in)
Length 56cm (22in)
Sleeve seam 43cm (17in)

Bold and bright

## Materials

Of St John's Double Knitting Wool, 10(12) 25g hanks in Peacock (M), 5(6) hanks in Kingcup (C), 3(4) hanks in Saxe, 4 hanks in Peony, 2(3) hanks each in Apple and Turquoise, 1(2) hanks each in Rust and Moorheather. (Yarn available from St John's Wools, PO Box 55, Parkside Mills, West Bowling, Bradford, BD5 8DZ.)
1 pair each of 3¼ and 4mm knitting needles.

## Tension

26 sts and 26 rows to 10cm (4in) over pattern on 4mm needles, or size required to obtain correct tension.

## Main part (worked in one piece to armholes)

Using 3¼mm needles and C cast on 200(235) sts.
Beg with a P row, work 4 rows in reverse st st.
* Using M and beg with a K row work 6 rows in st st.
Using C K 2 rows, P 1 row, K 1 row. *
Rep from * to * twice more. Change to 4mm needles.
*Next row:* Using M, K9(12), (inc in next st, K5) 30(35) times, inc in next st, K10(12). 231(271) sts.
*Next row:* Using M, P to end.
Cont in st st, working in patt from chart, until 75 rows have been worked in patt, ending with a K row.
*Divide for armholes*
*Next row:* P53(63), cast off 10, P105(125), including st on needle, cast off 10, P to end.
Keeping patt correct, cont on last 53(63) sts for right front.
*Next row:* K1, K2 tog, K to last 3 sts, sl 1, K1, psso, K1.
*Next row:* P1, P2 tog tbl, P to last 3 sts, P2 tog, P1.
Rep the last 2 rows 3 times more. 37(47) sts.
Keeping armhole edge straight, dec at front edge as before on next 6 rows, then on every 3rd row twice and every 4th row 4 times. 25(35) sts.
Cont without shaping until 121 rows *in all* have been worked in patt, ending with a K row. Work 1 row each in Peony, Turquoise, Rust and Kingcup, then cast off in Kingcup.
Return to the 105(125) sts for back; with right side facing rejoin yarn and cont in patt.
*Next row:* K1, K2 tog, K to last 3 sts, sl 1, K1, psso, K1.
*Next row:* P1, P2 tog tbl, P to last 3 sts, P2 tog, P1.
Rep the last 2 rows 3 times more. 89(109) sts.
Cont without shaping until work measures the same as front, ending with 4 rows of stripes as on front.
Cast off in Kingcup.

Key

- Peacock
- Apple
- Peony
- Saxe
- Rust
- Kingcup
- Moorheather
- Turquoise

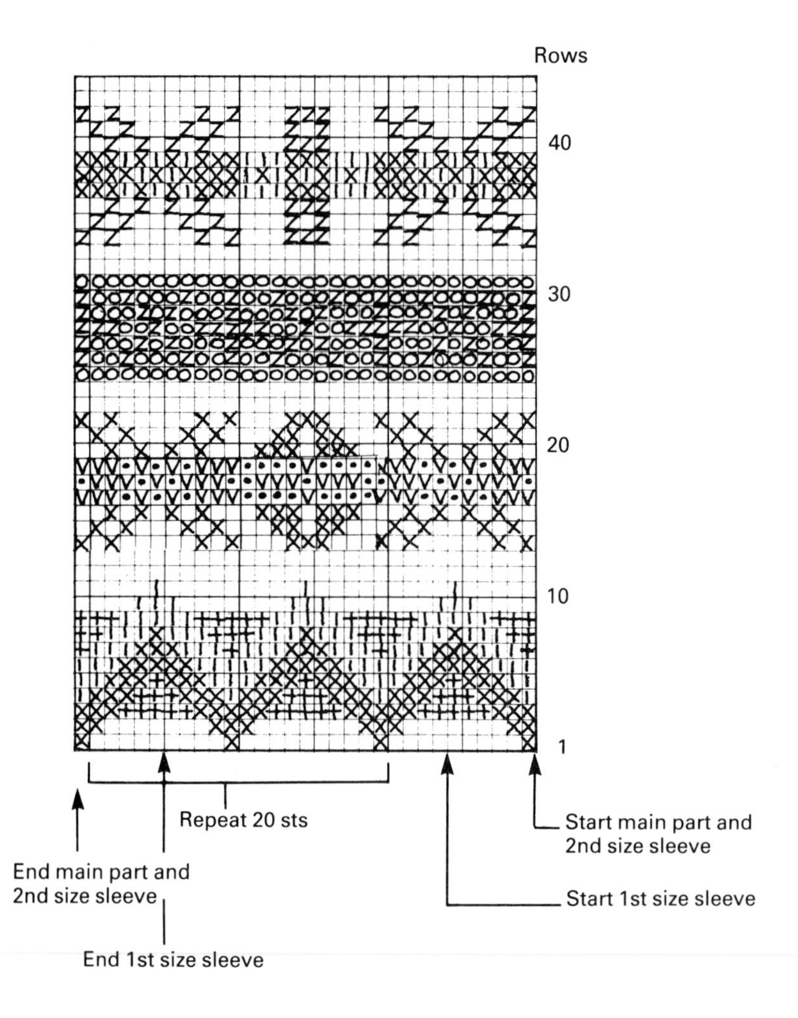


Return to the 53(63) sts for left front; with right side facing rejoin yarns and cont in patt.

*Next row:* K1, K2 tog, K to last 3 sts, sl 1, K1, psso, K1.

*Next row:* P1, P2 tog tbl, P to last 3 sts, P2 tog, P1.

Cont to match right front, reversing shaping as shown.

## Sleeves

With 4mm needles and M cast on 81(91) sts and, beg with a K row, work 2 rows in st st.

Cont in st st, working in patt from chart. Work 13th to 44th rows, rep 1st to 44th rows, then 1st to 31st rows again, thus ending with the same row as main part at armholes.

*Shape top*

*Next row:* Cast off 6, P to last 6 sts, cast off 5.

With right side facing rejoin yarns and cont in patt, cast off 2 sts at beg of next 2(4) rows. Dec one st at each end of next and every foll 3rd row until 41(45) sts rem, ending with a P row.

Cast off 2 sts at beg of next 4 rows, then 3 sts at beg of next 2 rows. Cast off rem 27(31) sts.

## Collar

With 3¼mm needles and M cast on 122 sts and work in garter st for 2cm (¾in).
*Next row:* K to last st, turn.
*Next row:* K to last st, turn.
*Next row:* K to last 2 sts, turn.
*Next row:* K to last 2 sts, turn.
Cont to work 1 st less on every row until there are 6 sts at each end; work 2 sts less on every row until 18 sts rem at each end, 3 sts less until 30 sts rem at each end, then 4 sts less until 50 sts rem at each end.
*Next row:* K to end.
K 1 row across all sts, then cast off loosely.

## Rouleau edging

Join shoulder seams. Sew straight edge of collar to neck edge.
With 3¼mm needles and C cast on 7 sts and, beg with a P row, cont in reverse st st until strip is long enough to go up front edge round collar and down other front. Cast off.

Make 2 more strips in the same way to fit round cuffs.

## Buttons (Make 10 pieces)

With 3¼mm needles and C cast on 5 sts and work 6 rows in reverse st st. Cast off.

## Button loops (Make 5)

With 3¼mm needles and C cast on 4 sts and work in reverse st st for 5cm (2in). Cast off.

## To make up

Press work according to instructions on ballband.
Join sleeve seams. Sew in sleeves.
Fold border in C at beg in half to inside and sl st.
Sew rouleau edging round front edges and collar, fold in half to inside and sl st. Sew edging to sleeves in the same way.
Sew button pieces tog in pairs and stitch 3 sides. Stuff with a small amount of yarn and join remaining seam. Sew buttons to left front edge and sew loops to right front edge to correspond.
Press seams.

# 18
# BOW-TIE *(colour plate 9)*

Combining Fair Isle and trompe l'oeil, a luxury sweater in pure wool for the very experienced knitter

**Measurements**
To fit bust 81–86cm (32–34in)
Length 53cm (21in)
Sleeve seam 43cm (17in)

**Materials**
Of Sunbeam Pure Wool Double Knitting, 5 50g balls in main colour Banana (A); 2 balls in each of first 3 contrast shades, Ice Blue, Lilac Dusk and Terra Cotta and 1 ball in each of 5 further contrast shades, Oyster, Pale Green, Zephyr, Blue Mist and Navy (these last 3 for the bow motif only).
1 pair each of 3¼ and 4mm knitting needles.

**Tension**
24 sts and 26½ rows to 10cm (4in) over Fair Isle pattern on 4mm needles, or size required to obtain tension.

**Back**
Using 3¼mm needles and A, cast on 108 sts. Work 5cm (2in) in K1 P1 rib.
Change to 4mm needles and work in patt from Chart 1, beginning with a K row, and repeating the 12 patt sts 9 times across. **
When all 59 rows of patt have been completed, work rows 1–20 again.
*Shape armholes*
Keeping continuity of patt, cast off 6 sts at beg of next 2 rows, then dec 1 st at each end of foll 6 rows to 84 sts. Cont without shaping in patt for a further 46 rows.

Ribbons

Cabled stripes

Impressionist

Carousel

Sweet and simple

Seashore

Fruit-drop

Candy stripes

Bow-tie

Pin-stripes

Merry-go-round

Frills and Fair Isle

More Frills and Fair Isle

Bouquet

Flowerbed

Flowerbed (detail)

*Shape neck*
Cast off 21 sts, K across centre 42 sts, cast off rem 21 sts. Leave centre 42 sts on stitch holder.

## Front

Work as given for back to **.
When all 59 rows of patt have been completed, work rows 1–15 again.
*Bow motif*
Cont in patt from Chart 2, beg with a K row, shaping armholes as indicated on Chart 1, for 42 rows.
*Shape neck*
*43rd row:* Patt 31 sts, turn and leave rem sts on spare needle. Cont in patt from Chart 2 on these first 31 sts only, dec 1 st at neck edge on every foll row to 21 sts. Work in patt from chart for a further 6 rows. Cast off.
With right side facing, slip centre 22 sts on to stitch holder. Rejoin yarn to rem 31 sts and patt to end from chart. Keeping continuity of patt as indicated on chart, work neck to match first side, reversing shapings.

## Sleeves

Using $3\frac{1}{4}$mm needles and A, cast on 50 sts. Work in K1 P1 rib for 5cm (2in), inc evenly by 34 sts on last row to 84 sts. Change to 4mm needles and work rows 43–57 from Chart 1, beg with a K row and rep the 12 patt sts 7 times across. Cont by working in patt from Chart 1 until rows 1–59 have been completed, then rep rows 1–20 again.
Continuing in patt from Chart 1, shape top by casting off 6 sts at beg of foll two rows, then dec by 1 st at each end of next 2 rows to 68 sts. Now dec by 1 st on every foll 3rd row to 60 sts, then at each end of every foll 4th row to 50 sts. Cont by casting off 1 st at each end of foll 5 alt rows, then at each end of every row to 28 sts. Cast off.

## Neckband

Join right shoulder seam.
Using $3\frac{1}{4}$mm needles and A, and with right side facing, pick up and K 17 sts down left front neck, K up centre front 22 sts from stitch holder, pick up and K 17 sts up right front neck and K up 42 sts from back neck. Work in K1 P1 rib for 6 rows. Cast off loosely in rib.

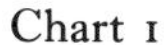

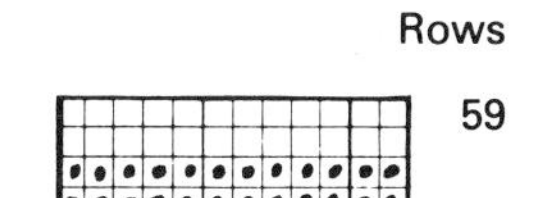
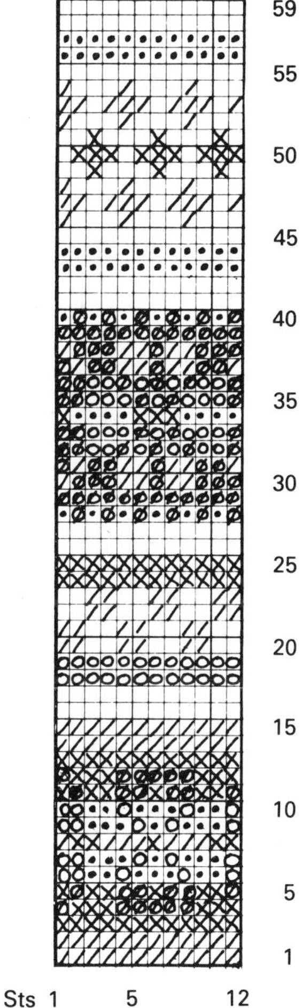


Key

- A (Banana)
- Ice Blue
- Lilac Dusk
- Terracotta
- Oyster
- Pale Green
- Navy
- Zephyr
- B Blue Mist

Chart 2

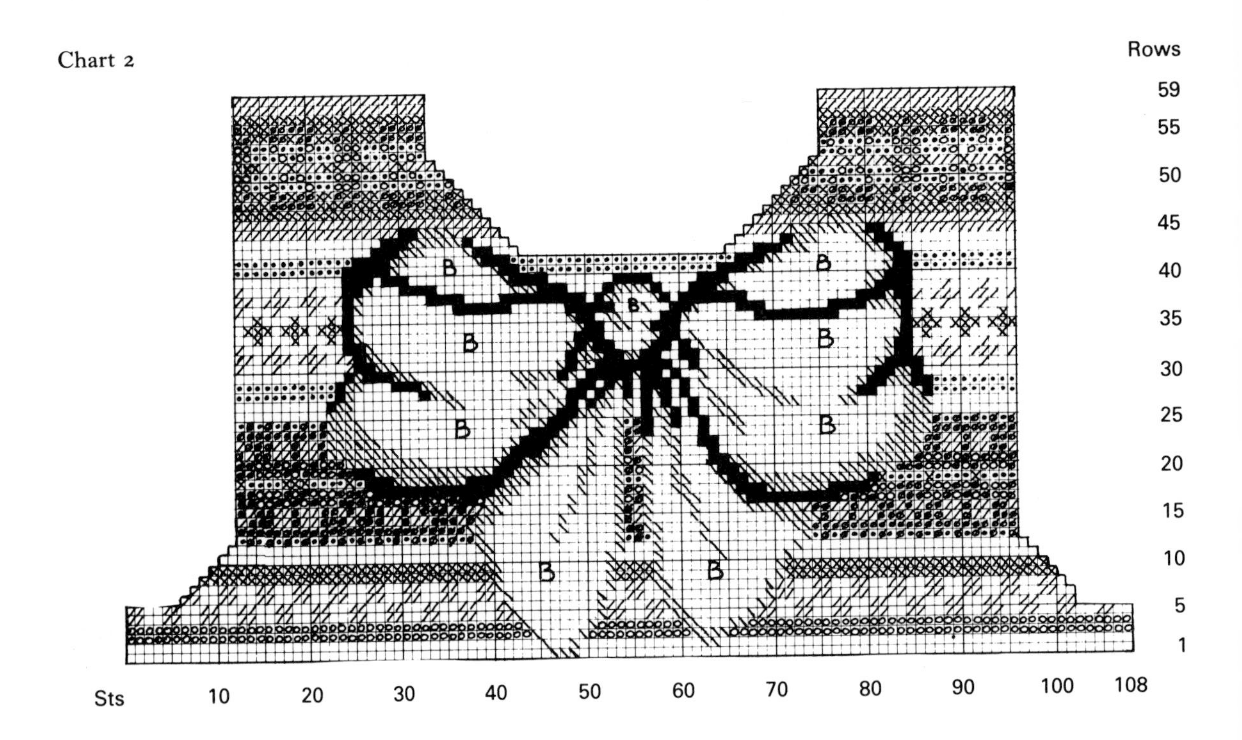


## To make up

Read and follow pressing instructions on ballband.
Join left shoulder seam and neckband. Join side and sleeve seams. Set in sleeves, gathering in any fullness at shoulder.

19

# PIN-STRIPES

*(colour plate 10)*

Wear your own pin-striped jacket to the office!
For the experienced knitter

**Measurements**
To fit bust 86–91cm (34–36in)
Length 51cm (20in)
Sleeve seam 43cm (17in)

**Materials**
Of Sirdar Talisman 4 ply, 8 50g balls in Clerical Grey (A); 4 balls in Silver Cloud (B); 1 ball in each of Viridian, Bottle, Festive Scarlet, Maroon and Black.
1 pair each of $2\frac{1}{2}$ and $3\frac{1}{4}$mm knitting needles.

**Tension**
$28\frac{1}{2}$ sts and 33 rows to 10cm (4in) over pattern on $3\frac{1}{4}$mm needles or size required to obtain correct tension.

**Back**
Using $2\frac{1}{2}$mm needles and A, cast on 129 sts. Work in rib thus:
*1st row:* K1, *P1, K1; rep from * to end.
*2nd row:* P1, *K1, P1; rep from * to end.
Rep these 2 rows for 2cm ($\frac{3}{4}$in), ending with a 2nd row and inc by 10 sts evenly across last row; 139 sts. **
Change to $3\frac{1}{4}$mm needles and joining in B, work in patt.
*1st row:* K3A, 1B, *4A, 1B; rep from * to end.
*2nd row:* *P1B, 4A; rep from * to last 4 sts, P1B, 3A.
These 2 rows form patt on back.
Cont in patt for a further 98 rows.
*Shape armholes*
Keeping continuity of patt, cast off 7 sts at beg of next 2 rows, then dec 1 st at each end of every foll row to 107 sts.

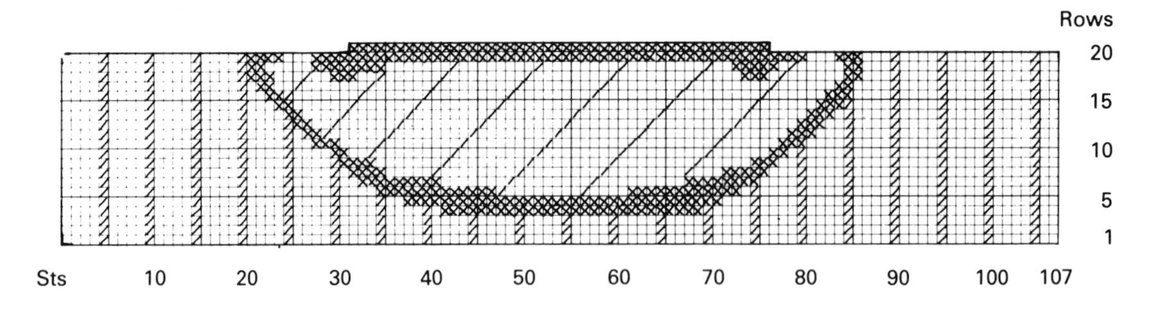


Chart 1

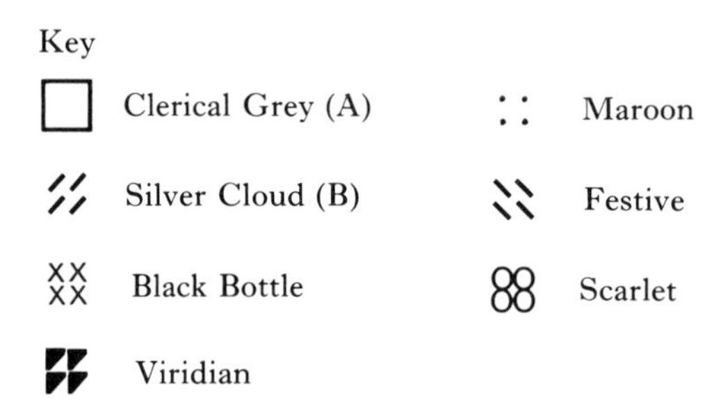


Cont in patt without shaping for a further 27 rows, then work back collar motif from Chart 1, reading odd rows K and even rows P.
When all 20 rows of chart have been completed, shape neck thus.
*21st row:* Cast off 31 sts, K across centre 45 sts in Black, cast off rem 31 sts.
Leave centre 45 sts on stitch holder.

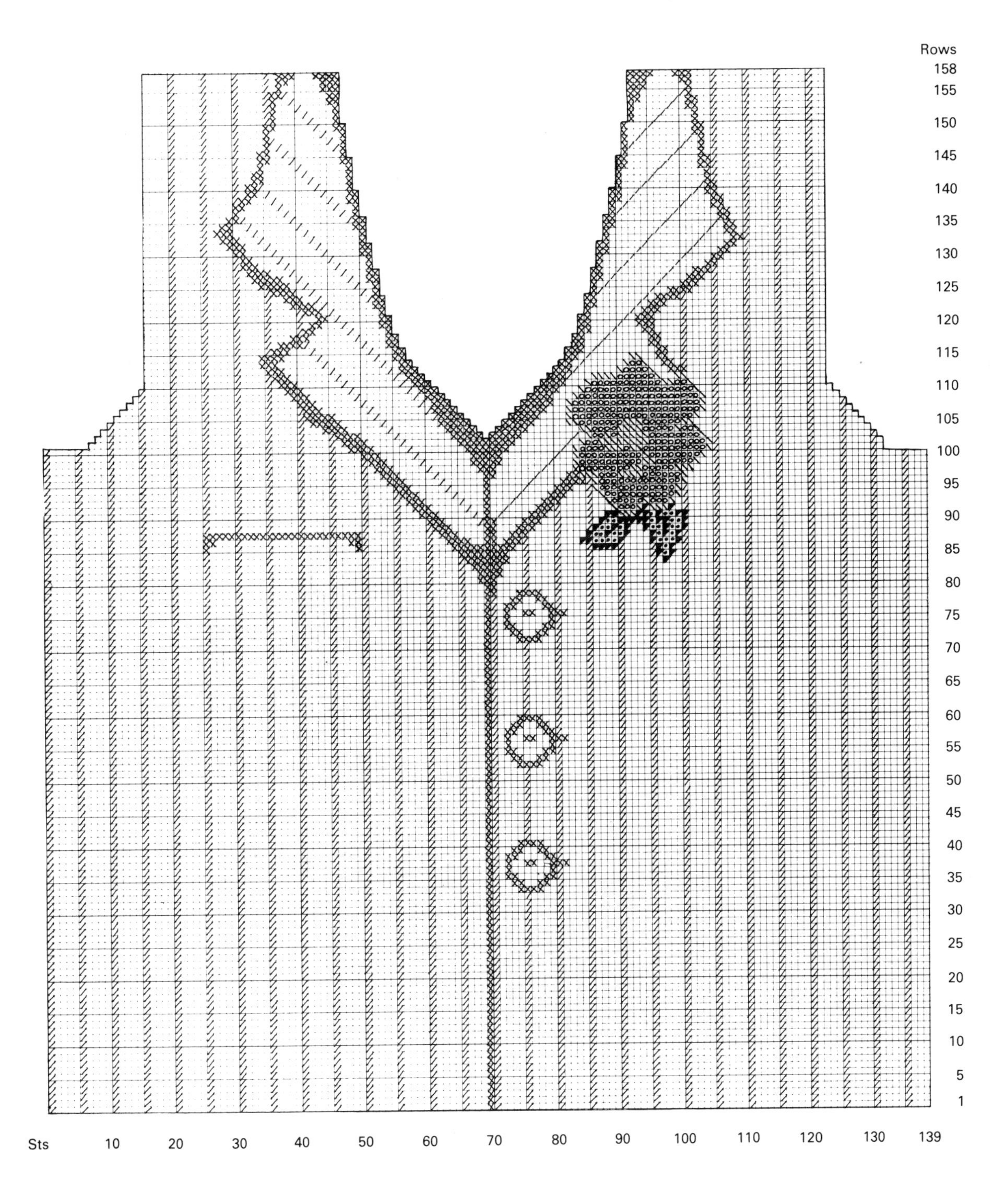
Rows
158
155
150
145
140
135
130
125
120
115
110
105
100
95
90
85
80
75
70
65
60
55
50
45
40
35
30
25
20
15
10
5
1
Sts
10
20
30
40
50
60
70
80
90
100
110
120
130
139

Chart 2

## Front

Work as given for back to **.

Change to $3\frac{1}{4}$mm needles and, joining in B and contrast shades as required, work in patt from Chart 2 for 100 rows, beg with a K row.

*Shape armhole*

Cast off 7 sts at beg of next 2 rows, maintaining continuity of patt as indicated on chart.

*Shape neck*

*Next row:* K2 tog, patt 60 sts, turn, leaving rem sts on spare needle.

Now cont on first 61 sts only, shaping neck and armholes as indicated on chart and maintaining patt continuity, until all 158 rows of chart have been completed. Cast off.

Slip centre st on to safety pin.

With right side facing rejoin yarn to rem 62 sts, patt 60 sts, K2 tog.

Cont shaping of neck and armhole to match first side, working patt as indicated on chart, until all 158 rows have been completed. Cast off.

## Sleeves

Using $2\frac{1}{2}$mm needles and A, cast on 49 sts. Work in rib as for back for 3cm ($1\frac{1}{4}$in), ending with a 2nd row.

Change to $3\frac{1}{4}$mm needles and joining in B, work in stripe patt as for back, inc 1 st at each end of 3rd and every foll 4th row to 95 sts. Cont without further shaping in patt until sleeve measures 43cm (17in) from beg, ending with a 2nd patt row.

*Shape top*

Cast off 5 sts at beg of next 2 rows. Keeping continuity of patt, dec 1 st at each end of every foll row to 75 sts, then at each end of every alt row to 45 sts. Now dec 1 st at each end of every row to 23 sts. Cast off.

## Neckband

Join right shoulder seam.

Using $2\frac{1}{2}$mm needles and Black and with right side facing, pick up and K 55 sts down left front neck, K up centre neck st from safety pin, marking that st with a contrast yarn, pick up and K 55 sts up right front neck and K across 45 sts from back neck.

Work rib as follows.

*1st row:* *P1, K1; rep from * to 2 sts at side of centre front marked st, P2 tog, K1, P2 tog tbl, (K1, P1) to end.

*2nd row:* *K1, P1; rep from * to 2 sts at side of centre front

marked st, K2 tog, P1, K2 tog tbl, (P1, K1) to end.
Rep these 2 rows twice more. Cast off in rib.

### To make up

Read and follow pressing instructions on ballband.
Join left shoulder and neckband seam.
Sew in sleeves, gathering in any fullness at shoulder. Join side and sleeve seams.

20

# MERRY-GO- ROUND

(*colour plate 11*)

Fun, eye-catching and simple to knit in double knitting yarn

### Measurements

To fit bust 81–86(91–97)cm (32–34[36–38]in)
Length 59cm (23in)
Sleeve seam 43cm (17in)

### Materials

Of Sunbeam Trophy Double Knitting in main colour (A), 9(10) 50g balls; 1 ball in contrast colour (B); scraps of 4 ply yarn in pink, red, blue, green, yellow, black and brown for dolls.
1 pair each of $3\frac{1}{4}$ and 4mm knitting needles.

### Tension

21 sts and 36 rows to 10cm (4in) over patt on 4mm needles, or size required to obtain correct tension.

### Back

Using $3\frac{1}{4}$mm needles and B, cast on 80(90) sts. Work 4 rows in K1 P1 rib.
Break off B and join A.
K one row.
Cont in K1 P1 rib in A until work measures 5cm (2in), ending with right side facing and inc evenly by 16 sts on last rib row. 96(106) sts.
Change to 4mm needles, and work in patt thus:
*1st row:* *K1, P1; rep from * to end (right side).
*2nd row:* *P1, K1; rep from * to end.
Rep the last 2 rows until work measures $30\frac{1}{2}$cm (12in) from beg, ending with right side facing.
Now work patt across yoke thus:

*1st row:* (K1, P1) for 44(48) sts, K8(10), (K1, P1) to end.
*2nd row:* (P1, K1) for 36(40) sts, P24(26), (P1, K1) to end.
*3rd row:* (K1, P1) for 30(34) sts, K36(38), (K1, P1) to end.
*4th row:* (P1, K1) for 28(32) sts, P40(42), (P1, K1) to end.
*5th row:* (K1, P1) for 26(30) sts, K44(46), (K1, P1) to end.
*6th row:* (P1, K1) for 24(28) sts, P48(50), (P1, K1) to end.
*7th row:* (K1, P1) for 22(26) sts, K52(54), (K1, P1) to end.
*8th row:* (P1, K1) for 20(24) sts, P56(58), (P1, K1) to end.
*9th row:* (K1, P1) for 18(22) sts, K60(62), (K1, P1) to end.
*10th row:* (P1, K1) for 16(20) sts, P64(66), (P1, K1) to end.
*11th row:* (K1, P1) for 14(18) sts, K68(70), (K1, P1) to end.
*12th row:* (P1, K1) for 12(16) sts, P72(74), (P1, K1) to end.
*13th row:* (K1, P1) for 10(14) sts, K76(78), (K1, P1) to end.
*14th row:* (P1, K1) for 8(12) sts, P80(82), (P1, K1) to end.
*15th row:* (K1, P1) for 8(12) sts, K80(82), (K1, P1) to end.
*16th row:* (P1, K1) for 6(10) sts, P84(86), (P1, K1) to end.
*17th row:* (K1, P1) for 6(10) sts, K84(86), (K1, P1) to end.
*18th row:* (P1, K1) for 6(10) sts, P84(86), (P1, K1) to end.
*19th row:* (K1, P1) for 6(10) sts, K84(86), (K1, P1) to end.
*20th row:* (P1, K1) for 4(8) sts, P88(90), (P1, K1) to end.
*21st row:* (K1, P1) for 4(8) sts, K88(90), (K1, P1) to end.**
Now repeat 20th and 21st rows until work measures 59cm (23½in), ending with right side facing.
*Shape shoulders*
*Next row:* Cast off 28(33) sts, K across next 40 sts, cast off rem 28(33) sts.
Cast off centre 40 sts.

## Front

Work as given for back to **, then rep rows 20 and 21 until work meaures 51cm (20in), ending with right side facing.
*Shape neck*
*Next row:* Patt 39(44), turn and leave rem sts on a spare needle. Keeping continuity of yoke stitch patt, dec 1 st at neck edge on next and every foll row to 28(33) sts, then cont without shaping until work measures the same as back to shoulders.
Cast off rem 28(33) sts.
Return to the sts on spare needle; with wrong side facing rejoin yarn and cast off centre 18 sts, patt to end.
Cont to match first side, reversing shaping.

## Sleeves

Using 3¼mm needles and B, cast on 40(42) sts. Work 4 rows in K1 P1 rib.

Break off B and join A. K one row.
Cont in K1 P1 rib in A until work measures 5cm (2in), ending with right side facing.
Change to 4mm needles and work in patt thus:
*1st row:* *K1, P1; rep from * to end (right side).
*2nd row:* *P1, K1; rep from * to end.
Cont in patt, inc 1 st at each end of next and every 6th row to 66(70) sts.
Now cont in patt without shaping until sleeve measures 43cm (17in) from beg.
Cast off loosely in patt.

## Collar

Using 3¼mm needles and A, cast on 119 sts.
*1st row:* K1, *P1, K1, rep from * to end.
*2nd row:* P1, *K1, P1, rep from * to end.
Change to 4mm needles and inc evenly by 30 sts across next row, maintaining rib patt as given for 1st and 2nd rows.
Now cont straight in rib until work measures 4cm (1½in) from beg, ending with right side facing.
Change to B.
K one row, then work 4 rows in rib in B.
Cast off loosely in rib.

## To make up

Read and follow pressing instructions on ballband.
Join shoulder seams. Set in sleeves. Join side and sleeve seams.
Sew on collar, using an oversew stitch.

## Dolls

Each doll is knitted separately and sewn on. A total of 8 dolls are needed.

### *Head*

Using 3¼mm needles and pink 4 ply yarn, cast on 4 sts. Work 4 rows st st, then inc by 1 st at each end of next and every foll row to 12 sts. Work 4 rows without shaping, then dec 1 st at each end of next and every foll row to 8 sts. Cast off.

### *Legs*

Using 3¼mm needles and black 4 ply yarn, cast on 2 sts. K 1 row, then inc by 1 st at each end of next row to 4 sts. Work 2 rows st st, then break off black yarn and join pink. Work in st st for 16 rows. Cast off. Make 2 legs for each doll.

*Arms*
Using 3¼mm needles and pink yarn, cast on 2 sts. K one row, then inc by 1 st at each end of next row to 4 sts. Work in st st for 7 more rows. Break off pink yarn and join coloured yarn to match dress or trouser colour as required. Work 6 more rows st st. Cast off. Make 2 arms thus for each doll.

*Dresses*
Using 3¼mm needles and coloured 4 ply yarn (blue, yellow, green, etc.), cast on 16 sts. Work 5 rows st st, then dec 1 st at each end of every row to 4 sts. Cast off.

*Trousers*
Using 3¼mm needles and coloured 4 ply yarn as for dresses, cast on 4 sts. K one row, then cont in st st, inc 1 st at each end of next and every foll alt row to 8 sts, then at each end of every foll 3rd row to 12 sts. P one row, then shape legs as follows:
*Next row:* K twice into first st, K5, turn, leaving rem sts on safety pin.
Working on first 6 sts only, cont in st st for 5 more rows, inc by 1 st at side edge on 3rd row. Cast off.
Rejoin yarn to 7 sts on safety pin. Cast off centre 2 sts, K to last st, knitting twice into last st.
Now work second trouser leg to match first, reversing shaping.

**To make up and attach dolls**
Sew up all leg and arm seams. Sew all dress seams, leaving hole at neck for insertion of head. Sew trouser legs around legs and stitch up back seam of trouser pieces to neck, leaving hole at neck for head.
Sew up head seam, gathering up top of head, inserting a small amount of pink yarn for stuffing and sewing threads on to dresses or trouser pieces as required. Stitch on arms, and sew legs into dresses.
Embroider faces on to dolls and using black or brown yarn, sew hair in position.
Tie a small amount of yarn around the waist of each doll.
Arrange dolls in circle around yoke of sweater, pin into position and then sew on at head, waist, arms and legs, loosely but firmly.

*Bows*
Make bows, if required, thus:
Measure approx 125cm (49in) of B, fold in two and knot both

ends together. Hook knotted end over door-handle, or ask a friend to hold it. Pull the length of yarn tight and insert a pencil between the length of yarn at the end opposite to the knotted end. Turn the pencil clockwise until both strands are tightly twisted together, then knot together both ends of the twisted skein. Use the resulting rope of yarn to tie into a bow. Make 9 bows, sewing them between the hands of each doll and one at the collar of the sweater.

# 21
# ICEBERG

A thick, thick sweater for mid-winter wear

**Measurements**
To fit bust 81(86,91)cm (32[34,36]in)
Length 56(57,58)cm (22[22½,23]in)
Sleeve seam 44cm (17½in)

Iceberg

## Materials

Of Hayfield Gaucho, 23(25,27) 50g balls.
1 pair each of $5\frac{1}{2}$ and $6\frac{1}{2}$mm knitting needles.
Cable needle.

## Tension

28 sts and 32 rows to 10cm (4in) over patt on $6\frac{1}{2}$mm needles.

## Back

Using $5\frac{1}{2}$mm needles cast on 82(90,98) sts.
*1st row:* K2, *P2, K2, rep from * to end.
*2nd row:* P2, *K2, P2, rep from * to end.
Rep these 2 rows for 5cm (2in), ending with a 1st row.
*Next row:* Rib 2(6,10), (inc in next st, rib 1, inc in each of next 2 sts, rib 1) 16 times, rib 0(4,8). 130(138,146) sts.
Change to $6\frac{1}{2}$mm needles and cont in patt thus:
1st row: K1, (sl next 4 sts on to a cable needle to front of work, K4, then K4 from cable needle) to last st, K1.
Beg with a P row work 3 rows in st st.
*5th row:* K5, (sl next 4 sts on to a cable needle to back of work, K4, then K4 from cable needle) to last 5 sts, K5.
Beg with a P row work 3 rows in st st.
These 8 rows form the patt and are rep throughout. Cont in patt until work measures approx 37cm ($14\frac{1}{2}$in) from beg, ending with a 4th patt row.
*Shape armholes*
Keeping patt correct, cast off 8 sts at beg of next 2 rows, then dec 1 st at each end of every row until 90(98,106) sts rem. Cont without shaping until armholes measure 19(20,21)cm ($7\frac{1}{2}$[$7\frac{3}{4}$,$8\frac{1}{4}$]in) from beg, ending with a P row.
*Shape shoulders*
*Next row:* Cast off 25(27,29), patt until 40(44,48) sts on right-hand needle, cast off rem 25(27,29) sts.
Leave centre sts on a holder.

## Front

Work as given for back until armholes measure 12(13,14)cm ($4\frac{3}{4}$[$5\frac{1}{4}$,$5\frac{1}{2}$]in), ending with a wrong side row.
*Shape neck*
*Next row:* Patt 37(39,41), turn and leave rem sts on a spare needle. Dec one st at neck edge on every row until 25(27,29) sts rem, then cont without shaping until armhole measures the same as on back, ending with a wrong side row. Cast off.

Return to the sts on spare needle; with right side facing, sl first 16(20,24) sts on to a holder, rejoin yarn and patt to end. Cont to match first side.

## Sleeves

Using $5\frac{1}{2}$mm needles cast on 30(38,38) sts and work in rib as on back for 5cm (2in), ending with a 1st row.
*Next row:* Rib 0(4,4), (inc in each of next 2 sts, rib 1) 10 times, rib 0(4,4). 50(58,58) sts.
Change to $6\frac{1}{2}$mm needles and cont in patt as on back, inc 1 st at each end of 3rd and every foll 4th row until there are 90(98,98) sts, then cont without shaping until sleeve measures 44cm ($17\frac{1}{2}$in) from beg, ending with a wrong side row.
*Shape top*
Keeping patt correct, cast off 8 sts at beg of next 2 rows, then 2 sts at beg of next 32(36,36) rows. Cast off rem 10 sts.

## Polo collar

Join right shoulder seam. With $5\frac{1}{2}$mm needles and right side facing pick up and K 13 sts down left front neck, K front neck sts, pick up and K 13 sts up right front neck, then K back neck sts. 82(90,98) sts.
*Next row:* P to end, inc 40 sts evenly across the row 122(130,138) sts.
Beg with a 1st row, cont in rib as on back for 24cm ($9\frac{1}{2}$in). Cast off loosely in rib.

## To make up

Do not press. Join left shoulder seam and collar. Sew in sleeves. Join side and sleeve seams.

# 22

# FRILLS AND FAIR ISLE

(*colour plate 12*)

Key

- Scarlet
- Pale Blue
- Purple
- Turquoise
- Khaki
- Tan
- Fuchsia Pink

Chart 1

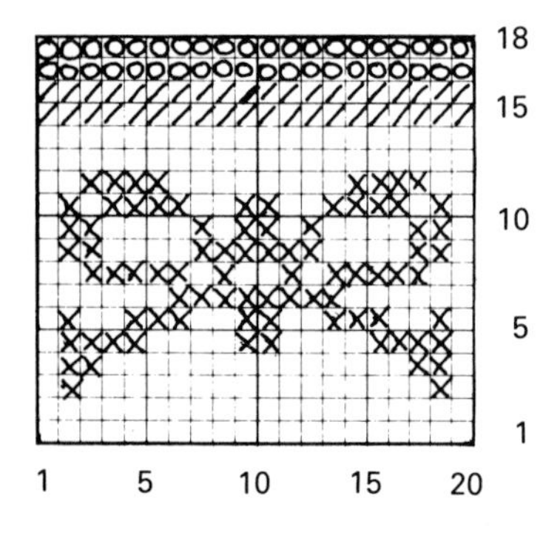


Chart 2

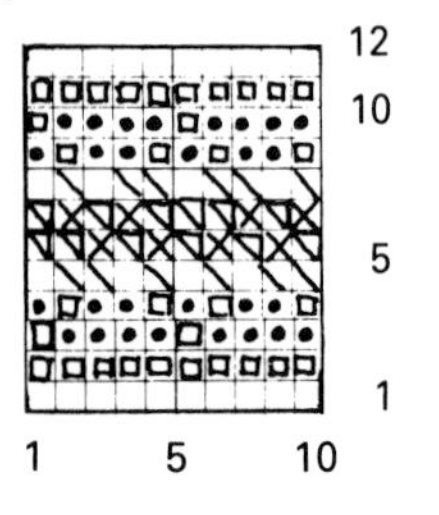


## Vivid colours in pure new wool

### Measurements

To fit bust 91–97cm (36–38in)
Length 64cm (25in)
Sleeve seam 43cm (17in)

### Materials

Of Shetland 2 ply Jumper yarn, 8oz Scarlet (93); 3oz in each of Pale Blue (14), and Bright Yellow (91); 2oz in each of Purple (44), Fuchsia Pink (52) and 1oz in Khaki (28), Cream (1a), Turquoise (71) and Tan (32).
(This yarn is available from Jamieson's Knitwear, 93–95 Commercial Street, Lerwick, Shetland, ZE1 0BD.)
1 pair each of $3\frac{1}{4}$ and $2\frac{3}{4}$mm knitting needles.

### Tension

29 sts and 31 rows to 10cm (4in) over pattern on $3\frac{1}{4}$mm needles, or size required to obtain correct tension.

### Back

Using $2\frac{3}{4}$mm needles and Scarlet (S), cast on 120 sts. Work 6cm ($2\frac{1}{2}$in) in K1 P1 rib, inc evenly by 20 sts across last row to 140 sts.
Change to $3\frac{1}{4}$mm needles and work in patt thus:
*1st–18th rows:* Work in patt from Chart 1, beg with a K row and repeating the 20 patt sts 7 times.
*19th–30th rows:* Work in patt from Chart 2, repeating the 10 patt sts 14 times.
*31st–49th rows:* Work in patt from Chart 3, repeating the 20 patt sts 7 times.
*50th–60th rows:* Work in patt from Chart 4, repeating the 10 patt sts 14 times.

*61st–68th rows:* Work in patt from Chart 5, repeating the 4 patt sts 35 times.
*69th–86th rows:* Work in patt from Chart 1.
*87th–105th rows:* Work in patt from Chart 3.
*106th–110th rows:* Work the first 5 rows in patt from Chart 4.
Now work a further 16 rows in patt from Chart 4, *at the same time* shaping armhole by casting off 7 sts at beg of next 2 rows, then dec 1 st at each end of every foll row to 118 sts.
*117th–128th rows:* Cont armhole shaping by dec 1 st at each end of every row to 100 sts, at the same time working in patt from Chart 2.
*129th–147th rows:* Work in patt from Chart 3.**
*148th–165th rows:* Work in patt from Chart 1.
*166th–173rd rows:* Work in patt from Chart 5.
Now work 2 rows st st in S, 2 rows st st in purple and 2 rows in yellow.
*Shape shoulders*
*Next row:* Cast off 28 sts, K across centre 44 sts, cast off remaining 28 sts.
Cast off centre 44 sts.

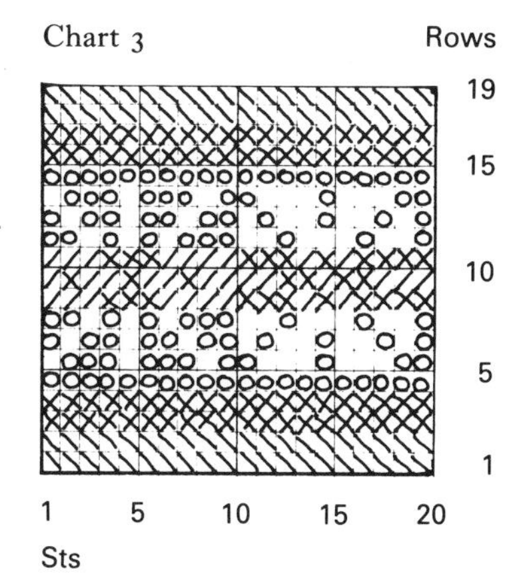


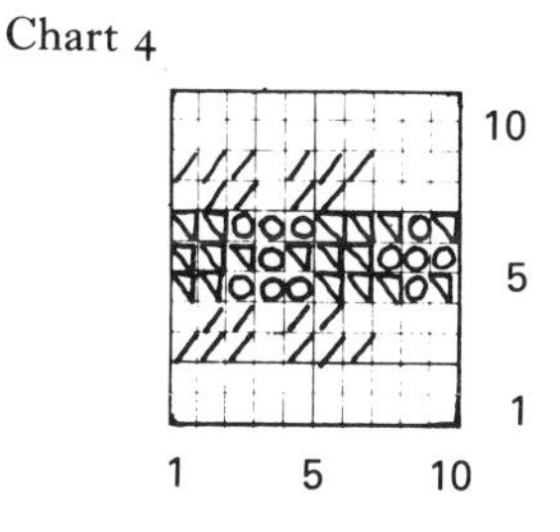


## Front
Work as given for back to **.
*148th row:* Work the first row of Chart 1.
Now cont in patt from Chart 1 and thereafter as given for back, *at the same time* shaping neck thus:
*149th row:* Patt 40, turn and leave rem sts on a spare needle.
Keeping continuity of patt, dec 1 st at neck edge on every row to 28 sts, then continue without shaping in patt to match back. Cast off.
Return to the sts on spare needle; rejoin yarn and cast off centre 20 sts, then patt across rem 40 sts.
Cont to match first side, reversing shapings.

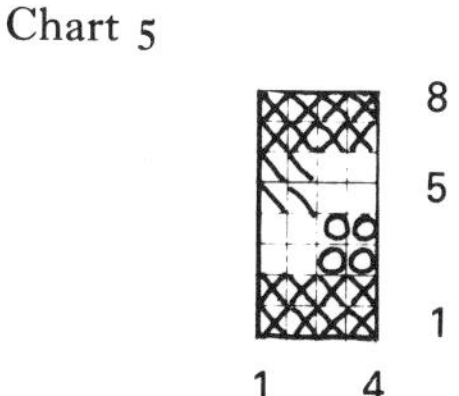


## Sleeves
Using $2\frac{3}{4}$mm needles and S cast on 50 sts and work 7cm ($2\frac{3}{4}$in) K1 P1 rib.
*Next row:* Work twice into every st, thus inc to 100 sts.
Change to $3\frac{1}{4}$mm needles and work in patt thus:
*1st–18th rows:* Work in patt from Chart 1, beg with a K row and repeating the 20 patt sts 5 times.
*19th–30th rows:* Work in patt from Chart 2, repeating the 10 patt sts 10 times.
*31st–49th rows:* Work in patt from Chart 3, repeating the 20 patt sts 5 times.

*50th–60th rows:* Work in patt from Chart 4, repeating the 10 patt sts 10 times.
*61st–68th rows:* Work in patt from Chart 5, repeating the 4 patt sts 25 times.
*69th–86th rows:* Work in patt from Chart 1, repeating the 20 patt sts 5 times.
*87th–105th rows:* Work in patt from Chart 3.
*106th–110th rows:* Work the first 5 rows in patt from Chart 4.
Now work a further 6 rows in patt from Chart 4, *at the same time* shaping top by casting off 5 sts at beg of next two rows, then dec 1 st at each end of foll 4 rows.
Continue in patt from Charts 2, 3, 1 and 5 in that order, at the same time continuing shaping by dec 1 st at each end of foll alt rows twice, 1 st at each end of foll 3rd rows 13 times, then at each end of every alt row 6 times.
Working the last 6 rows in st st stripes as for back and front, dec 1 st at each end of every row to 18 sts. Cast off.

## Collar

Using 2¾mm needles and S, cast on 420 sts. Work 4 rows K.
Change to cream and work 24 rows in st st.
*Next row:* *K3 tog; rep from * to end. 140 sts.
Work 4 rows K1 P1 rib. Cast off.

## To make up

Join shoulder seams, side seams and sleeve seams. Set in sleeves, pleating any extra fullness at the top of the sleeve. Sew collar to neck using a sl st.

23 & 24

# MORE FRILLS AND FAIR ISLE

(*colour plate 13*)

The same Fair Isle patterns, but with neckline variations

## Measurements

To fit bust 81–86(91–97)cm (32–34[36–38]in)
Length 63cm (25in)
Sleeve seam 43cm (17in)

Chart 1

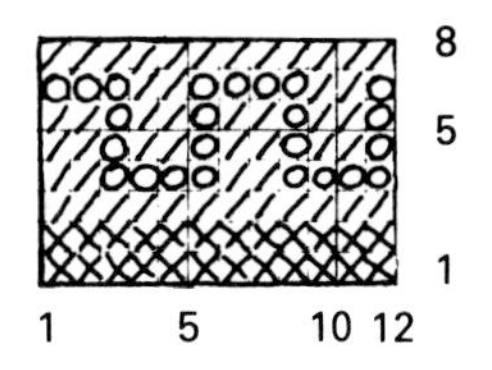


## Materials

Of Shetland 2 ply Jumper yarn, 4(5)oz of main shade (A); 3oz in 1st contrast shade, 2oz in each of 5 contrast shades, 1oz in last contrast shade, 2oz of Cream (1a) for V-neck version. (This yarn is available from Jamieson's Knitwear, 93–95 Commercial Street, Lerwick, Shetland, ZE1 0BD.)
1 pair each of $3\frac{1}{4}$ and $2\frac{3}{4}$mm knitting needles.
The colours used for the illustrated garments are as follows:

*V-neck sweater*
Main shade – Turquoise (71), 3oz of Pale Blue (14), 2oz in each of Purple (84), Yellow (46), Fuchsia (52), Lilac (49), Cream (1a), Pale Green (26), 1oz in Orange (73).

*Round-neck sweater*
Main shade – Fuchsia Pink (52), 3oz of Scarlet (93), 2oz in each of Purple (84), Royal Blue (17), Turquoise (71) and Bright Yellow (91), Dark Pink (68), 1oz in Orange (73).

Chart 2

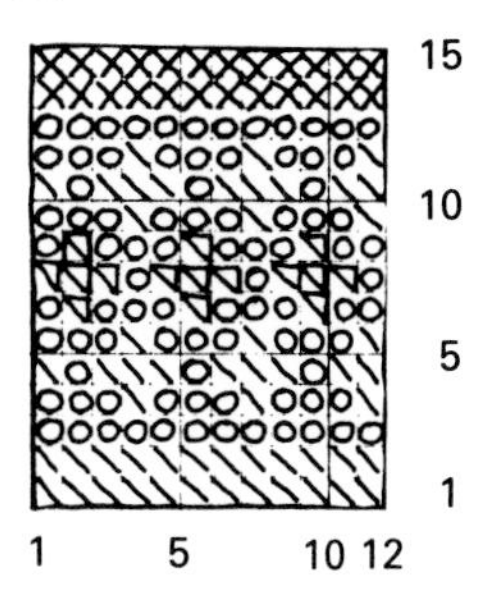


## Tension

29 sts and 31 rows to 10cm (4in) over pattern on $3\frac{1}{4}$mm needles, or size required to obtain correct tension.

## Back

Using $2\frac{3}{4}$mm needles and A, cast on 132(144) sts. Work 5cm (2in) K1 P1 rib.

Chart 3

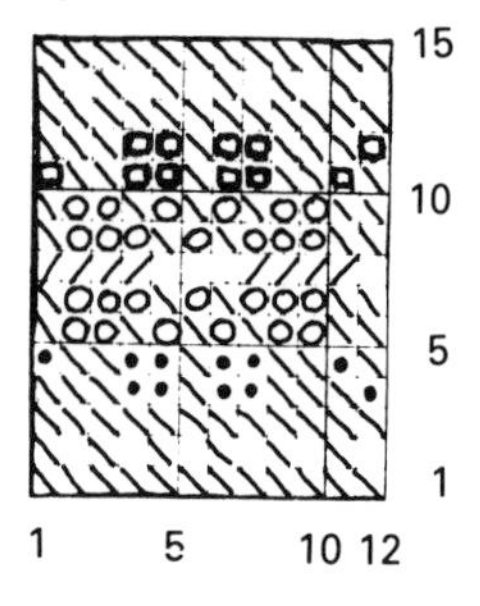


Chart 4

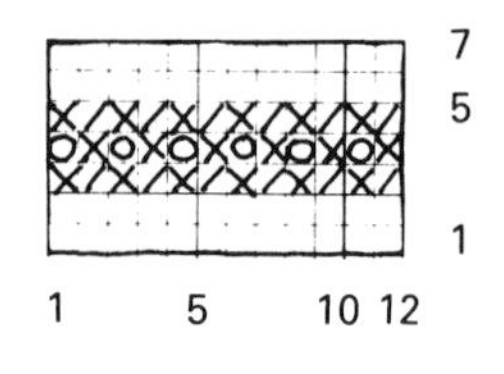


Chart 5

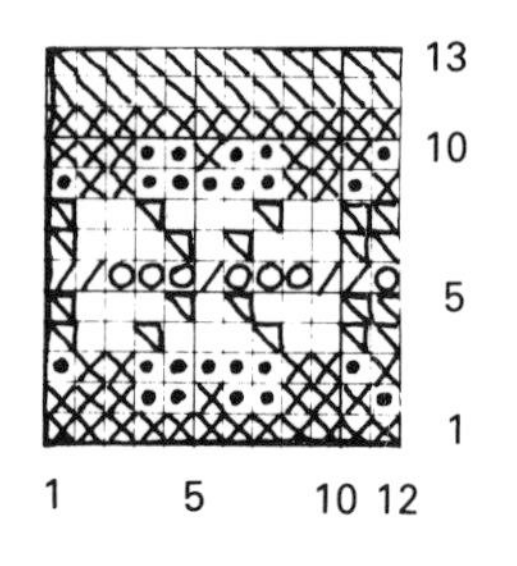


Change to 3¼mm needles and work in pattern thus:
*1st–8th rows:* Work in patt from Chart 1, beg with a K row and repeating the 12 patt sts 11(12) times across.
*9th–23rd rows:* Work in patt from Chart 2.
*24th–38th rows:* Work in patt from Chart 3.
*39th–45th rows:* Work in patt from Chart 4.
*46th–58th rows:* Work in patt from Chart 5.
*59th–73rd rows:* Work in patt from Chart 2.
*74th–81st rows:* Work in patt from Chart 1.
*82nd–96th rows:* Work in patt from Chart 3.
*97th–109th rows:* Work in patt from Chart 5.
*110th–117th rows:* Work in patt from Chart 1.**
*118th–139th rows:* Work in patt from Chart 4, then from Chart 2, *at the same time shaping armholes* by casting off 6 sts at the beg of 118th and 119th rows, then dec 1 st at each end of every row to 96(108) sts.
Cont without further shaping thus:
*140th–147th rows:* Work in patt from Chart 1.
*148th–154th rows:* Work in patt from Chart 4.
*155th–169th rows:* Work in patt from Chart 2.
*170th–177th rows:* Work in patt from Chart 1.
Break off all contrast shades and cont in A only, shaping shoulders by casting off 14(16) sts at the beg of next two rows, then cast off 13(17) sts at beg of foll two rows. Cast off rem 42 sts.

## Front

Work exactly as given for back to **.

### *Round neck version*

Cont as given for back to 162nd row, then, continuing in patt as given for back, *shape neck* thus:
*Next row:* Patt 36(42) sts, turn and leave rem sts on spare needle. Working on first 36(42) sts only, cont in patt, dec 1 st at neck edge on next and every foll row to 27(33) sts.
Cont without shaping to 177th row, then shape shoulders by casting off 14(16) sts at armhole edge on next row; work one row in A then cast off rem 13(17) sts. Return to the sts on the spare needle; rejoin yarn and cast off centre 24 sts, then patt across rem sts. Cont to match first side, reversing shapings.

### *V-neck version*

Work 118th row as given for back, casting off 6 sts at beg of row for armhole shaping.

*119th row:* Cast off first 6 sts, patt across next 60(66) sts, turn, leaving rem sts on spare needle.
Now, keeping continuity of patt as given for back, dec 1 st at neck edge on next and every foll alt row 11 times, then dec 1 st at neck edge on every 3rd row 10 times, *at the same time* shaping armhole by casting off 1 st at armhole edge on every row 12 times.
Cont in patt as given for back to 177th row, then break off all contrast shades and continue in A only, shaping shoulders by casting off 14(16) sts at armhole edge on next row. Work one row in A, then cast off rem 13(17) sts.
Return to the sts on the spare needle; rejoin yarn and patt across. Now work to match first side, reversing shapings.

## Sleeves

Using 2¾mm needles and A, cast on 43 sts. Work 5cm (2in) K1 P1 rib, working twice into each st on the final rib row, thus inc to 96 sts.
Change to 3¼mm needles and work in patt exactly as given for back for 118 rows, but repeating the 12 patt sts 8 times across.
When 118 rows of patt have been worked, *shape top* thus:
Cont in patt as given for back to 177th row, at the same time shaping top by casting off 5 sts at beg of next 2 rows, 3 sts at beg of foll 2 rows then dec 1 st at each end of every row to 74 sts. Now dec 1 st at each end of every alt row to 70 sts, then at each end of every 3rd row to 52 sts. Dec 1 st at each end of every alt row to 44 sts, then at each end of every row to 14 sts.
The last 3 rows should be worked in A. Cast off.

## Collar

*Round neck version*
*Back:* Using 3¼mm needles and A, cast on 132 sts. Work 4 rows K. Next work in patt from Chart 4, beg with a K row, then, when all 7 patt rows have been completed, work in patt from Chart 5. Break off all contrast shades.
*Next row:* *K3 tog; rep from * to end; 44 sts.
Work 4 rows in K1 P1 rib. Cast off.
*Front:* Using 3¼mm needles and A cast on 192 sts. Work 4 rows K. Next work in patt from Chart 4 for 7 rows, beg with a K row. Now work in patt from Chart 5. Break off all contrast shades.

*Next row:* *K3 tog; rep from * to end. 64 sts. Work 4 rows K1 P1 rib. Cast off.

*V-neck version*

*Frill – right side:* Using 2¾mm needles and A cast on 498 sts. Work 4 rows K.

Change to cream yarn. P one row.

*Next row:* Slip first 10 sts on spare needle, K to end.

*Next row:* P to last 10 sts, slip these on to spare needle.

Repeat these two rows a further 8 times.

*Next row:* Place 200 sts on spare needle from main needle; work across all 498 sts thus: *K3 tog; rep from * to end of row. 166 sts. Leave these on a spare needle.

*Frill – left side:* Using 2¾mm needles and A cast on 252 sts and work 4 rows K. Change to cream yarn and work 21 rows, beg with a P row.

*Next row:* *K3 tog; rep from * to end; 84 sts.

Now put 160 sts from spare needle on the same needle as the 84 sts. 244 sts.

Work 4 rows K1 P1 rib across all sts. Cast off.

## To make up

Join shoulder seams. Sew up side and sleeve seams; set in sleeves.

*Round neck version*

Sew front and back collar pieces together, and then stitch to neck using a slip stitch.

*V-neck version*

Sew up seam between right and left frills. Tack collar in position, with bottom edge between 24th and 26th rows of front. Then stitch down to front and around neck, using a sl st.

25

# FERN

A lace sweater in 4 ply wool for the confident knitter

## Measurements

To fit bust 81–86(91–97)cm (32–34[36–38]in)
Length 54cm (21in)
Sleeve seam to fit 43cm (17in)

## Materials

Of Sunbeam 4 ply Pure New Wool, 9(10) 50g balls.
1 pair each of 2¾ and 3¼mm knitting needles.

## Tension

29 sts and 38½ rows to 10cm (4in) over fern stitch pattern on 3¼mm needles, or size required to obtain correct tension.

## Back

Using 2¾mm needles cast on 137(149) sts.
*1st row:* K1, *P1, K1, rep from * to end.
*2nd row:* P1, *K1, P1, rep from * to end.
Rep these 2 rows for 2cm (¾in), ending with a 2nd row.
Change to 3¼mm needles and work in Vandyke Border pattern as follows:
*1st row:* K2, *K1, wf, K2 tog tbl, K7, K2 tog, wf, rep from * to last 3 sts, K3.
*2nd row:* K2, *P3, K7, P2, rep from * to last 3 sts, P1, K2.
*3rd row:* K2, *K2, wf, K2 tog tbl, K5, K2 tog, wf, K1, rep from * to last 3 sts, K3.
*4th row:* K2, *P4, K5, P3, rep from * to last 3 sts, P1, K2.
*5th row:* K2, *K1, (wf, K2 tog tbl) twice, K3, (K2 tog, wf) twice, rep from * to last 3 sts, K3.
*6th row:* K2, *P5, K3, P4, rep from * to last 3 sts, P1, K2.
*7th and 11th rows:* K2, *K2, (wf, K2 tog tbl) twice, K1, (K2

tog, wf) twice, K1, rep from * to last 3 sts, K3.

Fern (*opposite*)

*8th row:* K2, *P6, K1, P5, rep from * to last 3 sts, P1, K2.
*9th row:* K2, *K1, (wf, K2 tog tbl) twice, wf, sl 1, K2 tog, psso, wf, (K2 tog, wf) twice, rep from * to last 3 sts, K3.
*10th row:* K2, *K2, P9, K1, rep from * to last 3 sts, K3.
*12th row:* K2, *K2, P9, K1, rep from * to last 3 sts, K3.
*13th row:* K2, *K3, wf, K2 tog tbl, wf, sl 1, K2 tog, psso, wf, K2 tog, wf, K2, rep from * to last 3 sts, K3.
*14th row:* K2, *K4, P5, K3, rep from * to last 3 sts, K3.
*15th row:* K2, *K4, wf, K2 tog tbl, K1, K2 tog, wf, K3, rep from * to last 3 sts, K3.
*16th row:* K2, *K5, P3, K4, rep from * to last 3 sts, K3.
*17th row:* K2, *K5, wf, sl 1, K2 tog, psso, wf, K4, rep from * to last 3 sts, K3.
*18th row:* K.
Rep these 18 patt rows twice more.
Change to 2¾mm needles and work 3cm (1¼in) in K1 P1 rib as given for back edge, ending with a 2nd row and dec evenly by 5 sts along last row, to 132(144) sts.
Change to 3¼mm needles and work in fern stitch pattern as follows:
*1st row:* K5, *K2 tog, wf, K1, wf, sl 1, K1, psso, K7, rep from * to last 7 sts, K2 tog, wf, K5.
*2nd and every alt row:* K1, P to last st, K1.
*3rd row:* K4, *K2 tog, K1, wf, K1, wf, K1, sl 1, K1, psso, K5, rep from * to last 8 sts, K2 tog, K1, wf, K5.
*5th row:* K3, *K2 tog, K2, wf, K1, wf, K2, sl 1, K1, psso, K3, rep from * to last 9 sts, K2 tog, K2, wf, K5.
*7th row:* K2, *K2 tog, K3, wf, K1, wf, K3, sl 1, K1, psso, K1, rep from * to last 10 sts, K2 tog, K3, wf, K5.
*9th row:* K1, K2 tog, *K4, wf, K1, wf, K4, sl 1, K2 tog, psso, rep from * to last 9 sts, K4, wf, K5.
*11th row:* K2, *wf, sl 1, K1, psso, K7, K2 tog, wf, K1, rep from * to last 10 sts, wf, sl 1, K1, psso, K8.
*13th row:* K2, *wf, K1, sl 1, K1, psso, K5, K2 tog, K1, wf, K1, rep from * to last 10 sts, wf, K1, sl 1, K1, psso, K7.
*15th row:* K2, *wf, K2, sl 1, K1, psso, K3, K2 tog, K2, wf, K1, rep from * to last 10 sts, wf, K2, sl 1, K1, psso, K6.
*17th row:* K2, *wf, K3, sl 1, K1, psso, K1, K2 tog, K3, wf, K1, rep from * to last 10 sts, wf, K3, sl 1, K1, psso, K5.
*19th row:* K2, *wf, K4, sl 1, K2 tog, psso, K4, wf, K1, rep from * to last 10 sts, wf, K4, sl 1, K1, psso, K4.
*20th row:* K1, P to last st, K1.
Rep these patt rows 2 more times, then work rows 1–16 inc once.
*Shape armholes*, keeping continuity of patt.

Cast off 6 sts at beg of next 2 rows, then dec by 1 st at each end of foll 12 rows to 96(108) sts.**
Work straight in patt for a further 50 rows.
*Shape shoulders*
Cast off 22(28) sts, slip centre 52 sts on to spare needle, cast off rem 22(28) sts.

## Front

Work as given for back to **, then work 18 rows.
*Shape neck*, keeping continuity of patt.
*Next row:* Patt 37(43) sts, turn and leave rem sts on a spare needle. Dec 1 st at neck edge on next 15 rows to 22 sts, then cont until work measures the same as back to shoulders.
Cast off rem 22 sts.
Return to the sts on spare needle; slip centre 22 sts on to stitch holder, rejoin yarn to rem 37(43) sts, patt to end. Work to match first side, reversing shapings.

## Sleeves

Using 2¾mm needles cast on 48(60) sts.
Work in K1 P1 rib for 9cm (3½in).
Change to 3¼mm needles and work in fern st patt, inc 1 st at each end of next and every foll 6th row to 84(96) sts, then cont in patt without shaping until a total of 7 patt repeats have been worked from end of ribbing. Work rows 1–16 inclusive in patt.
*Shape top*
Cast off 6(8) sts at beg of next 2 rows.
Dec 1 st at each end of next and foll 4(6) rows, then at each end of every 3rd row to 28(32) sts, then at each end of every row to 10 sts. Cast off.

## Neckband

Join right shoulder seam.
Using 2¾mm needles and with right side facing, pick up and K 21 sts down left side neck, K up 22 sts from centre front, pick up and K 21 sts up right side neck and K up 52 sts from back. Work 10 rows K1 P1 rib. Cast off loosely in rib.

## To make up

Read pressing instructions on ballband. Join left shoulder and neckband seam. Join side and sleeve seams. Set in sleeves.

# 26
# BOUQUET
*(colour plate 14)*

## A floral motif on Fair Isle: a project for the experienced knitter

### Measurements
To fit bust 91–97cm (36–38in)
Length 57cm ($22\frac{1}{2}$in)
Sleeve seam 43cm (17in)

### Materials
Of Sunbeam Pure New Wool DK, 4 50g balls in Palm (M); 2 balls each in Banana (C), Aran, Terracotta and Navy; 1 ball each in Ice Blue, Zephyr, Blue Mist, Pale Green and Lilac Dust.
1 pair each of $3\frac{1}{4}$ and 4mm knitting needles.

### Tension
25 sts and 25 rows to 10cm (4in) over Fair Isle on 4mm needles.

### Back
Using $3\frac{1}{4}$mm needles and C cast on 101 sts.
*1st row:* K1, *P1, K1, rep from * to end.
*2nd row:* P1, *K1, P1, rep from * to end.
Rep these 2 rows once more. Break off C, join in M and K 1 row, then cont in rib until work measures 5cm (2in) from beg, ending with a 1st row.
*Next row:* Rib 3, inc in next st, (rib 4, inc in next st) 19 times, rib 2. 121 sts.
Change to 4mm needles and work 2 rows in st st.
Cont in st st, work in patt from charts, reading K rows from right to left and P rows from left to right. Work Charts 1, 2, 3, 4 and 5, then work 2 rows in M, ending with a K row.
Work the 38 rows of flower motif pattern from Chart 6, then P 1 row in M.

Key

Palm
Banana
Lilac Dusk
Terracotta
Pale Green
Navy
Zephyr
Ice Blue
A Aran
BM Blue Mist
BB Make bobble in Pale Green on this stitch thus: K 5 sts in next st, turn, P5, turn, K5, turn, P5, turn K5 tog.

Chart 1

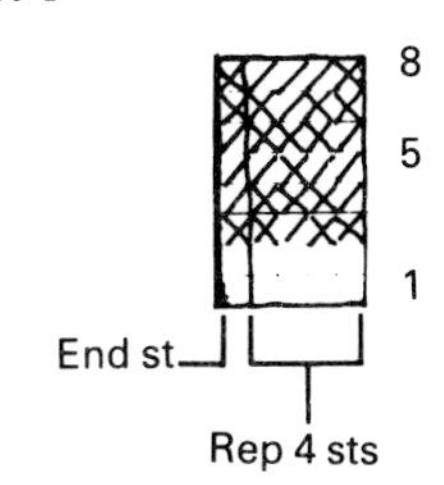

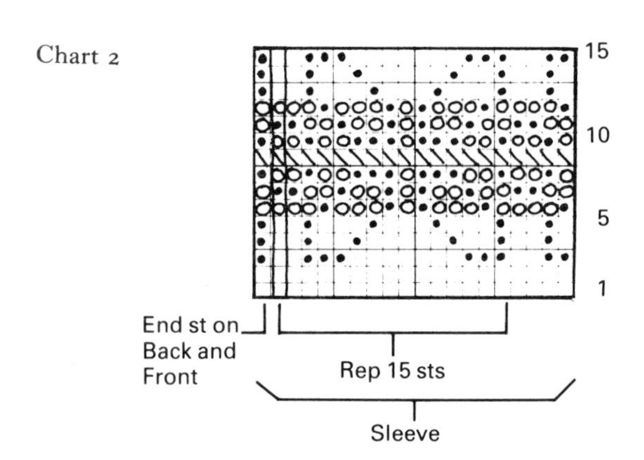


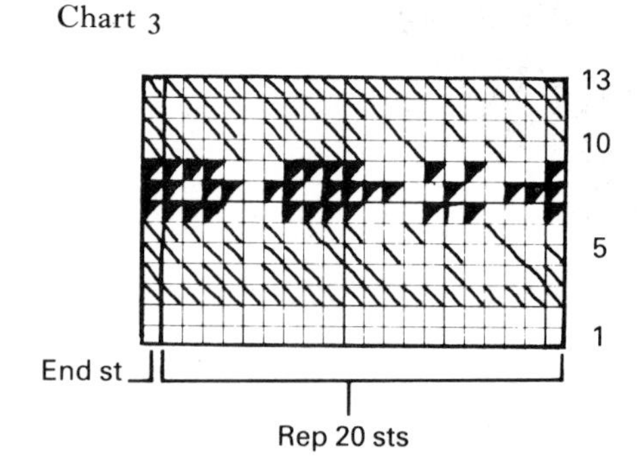


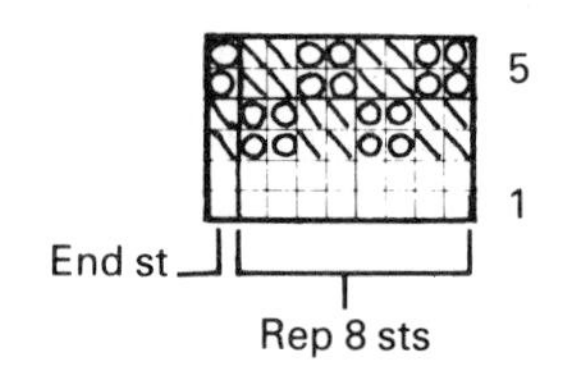


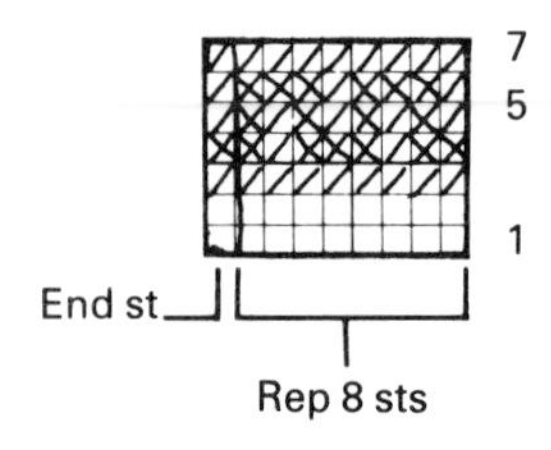


*Shape armholes*
Cont in patt as at beginning. Cast off 6 sts at beg of first 2 rows; dec 1 st at each end of every row until 87 sts rem, then cont without shaping until 49 rows of patt have been completed from beginning of armholes.
*Shape shoulders*
*Next row:* Cast off 23, P until 41 sts on right-hand needle, cast off rem 23 sts. Leave the centre sts on a holder.

**Front**
Work as given for back until 20 rows less than back to shoulders, ending with a K row.
*Shape neck*
*Next row:* P33, turn and leave rem sts on a spare needle. Dec one st at neck edge on every row until 23 sts rem, then cont without shaping until the 4 rows of patt have been completed. Cast off.
Return to the sts on spare needle; with wrong side facing sl first 21 sts on to a holder, rejoin yarns and P to end. Cont to match first side.

**Sleeves**
Using 3¼mm needles and C cast on 41 sts and work 4 rows in rib as on back. Break off C, join in M and K 1 row, then cont in rib until work measures 5cm from beg, ending with a 1st row.
*Next row:* P1, P twice into every st to end. 81 sts.
Change to 4mm needles and cont in st st, work 2 rows in C, 2 rows in Pale Green. Work the first 49 rows as on back, rep Charts 2, 3, 4 and 5 then K1 row in M.

Chart 6

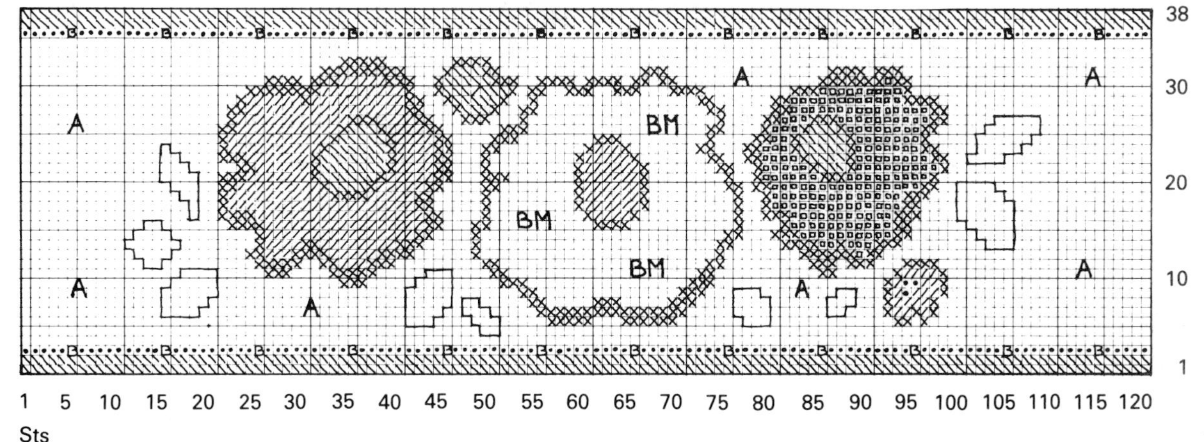


*Shape top*

Working the first 49 rows again, cast off 6 sts at beg of first 2 rows, then P 1 row. Dec one st at each end of next and foll 3 alt rows, at each end of every 4th row 5 times, at each end of every alt row 5 times, then at each end of every row until 25 sts rem. Cast off.

## Neckband

Join right shoulder seam. Using $3\frac{1}{4}$mm needles and M and with right side facing, pick up and K 20 sts down left front neck, K front neck sts, pick up and K 19 sts up right front neck, then K back neck sts. 101 sts.

Beg with a 2nd row, work 4 rows in rib as at beg. Join in C and P 1 row, then rib 2 rows.

*Next row:* K1, (wf, K2 tog) to end.

Work 2 more rows in rib. Break off C, rejoin M, P 1 row, then rib 4 rows. Cast off loosely in rib.

## To make up

Press work according to instructions on ballband.

Join left shoulder seam and neckband. Fold neckband in half to inside and sl st. Sew in sleeves. Join side and sleeve seams. Press seams.

27

# PINK AND PATTERNED

In Fair Isle, for the experienced knitter

**Measurements**
To fit bust 84–89(91–97)cm (33–35[36–38]in)
Length 61cm (24in)
Sleeve seam 44cm(17½in)

**Materials**
Of Hayfield Brig Double Knitting wool, 6(7) 50g balls in main colour (M), 2(2) balls in each of 5 contrast shades (A, B, C, D and E).
1 pair each of 3¼ and 4mm knitting needles.
2 buttons.

**Tension**
25 sts and 27 rows over pattern to 10cm (4in) on 4mm needles, or size required to obtain correct tension.

**Back**
With 3¼mm needles and D cast on 101(111) sts.
*1st row:* K1, *P1, K1, rep from * to end.
*2nd row:* P1, *K1, P1, rep from * to end.
Repeat these 2 rows once more.
Break off D, join in M and cont in rib until work measures 5cm (2in) from beginning, ending with a 2nd row and inc by 20 sts evenly across last row to 121(131) sts.
Change to 4mm needles and, beg with a K row, work 2 rows in st st, then cont in st st, working in patt from chart until 96 rows have been worked in patt.
*Shape armholes*
Keeping patt correct, cast off 5(7) sts at beg of next 2 rows, then dec one st at each end of next 7(8) rows. ** 97(101) sts.
Cont without shaping for 41(40) rows, ending on 40th row of chart. Work 2 rows in B and one in A.

Pink and patterned (*opposite*)

Key

M Main colour

A Rustic Brick

B Gold

C Blush Pink

D Cactus

E Old Rose

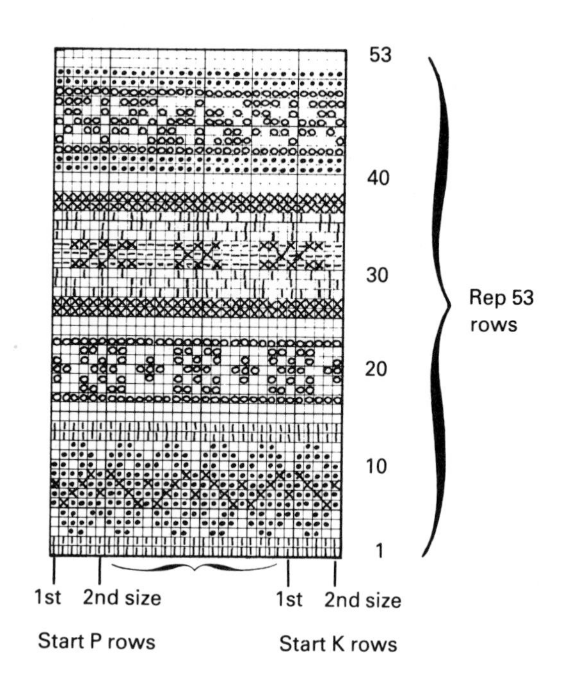


*Shape shoulders*

*Next row:* Using A, cast off 29(30) sts, P to last 29(30) sts, cast off to end. Leave centre 39(41) sts on a stitch holder.

## Front

Work as given for back to **, then work 13(12) rows.

*Divide for front opening*

*Next row:* K45(47)B, turn and leave rem sts on a spare needle.

*Next row:* With M, cast on 7 sts, K these 7 sts, then P to end in B.

*Next row:* K in patt to last 6 sts, K6M.

Cont as set, work 12 more rows, ending at neck edge.

*Shape neck*

Cast off 12(13) sts at beg of next row, then dec 1 st at neck edge on every row until 29(30) sts rem. Cont without shaping until work measures the same as back to shoulder, ending with a K row. Cast off. Return to the sts on spare needle; with right side facing K7M, then K to end in B.

*Next row:* P in patt to last 7 sts, K7M.

Next cont as set, working 4 more rows.

*Next row:* With M, K3, cast off 2, K2, then K to end in patt.

*Next row:* Work as set, casting on 2 sts over those cast off.

Cont to match first side, reversing shaping and working a 2nd buttonhole on 6th row above first.

## Sleeves

Using 3¼mm needles and D, cast on 51 sts and work 4 rows in rib as on back. Break off D, join in M and cont in rib until work measures 5cm (2in) from beg, ending with a 1st row.
*Next row:* P1, work twice into each st to end. 101 sts.
Change to 4mm needles and cont in st st; work 2 rows each in M, B, A, D and M, then cont in patt from chart for 96 rows.

*Shape top*

Keeping patt correct, cast off 8 sts at beg of next 2 rows. Dec 1 st at each end of next 7 rows, at each end of every 3rd row 9 times, then at each end of every alt row until 39 sts remain, ending with 40th row of chart.
*Next row:* With B, K2 tog to last st, K1. 20 sts.
*Next row:* With B, P2 tog to end. 10 sts.
*Next row:* With A, K2 tog to end. 5 sts.
Cast off purlwise.

## Collar

Join shoulder seams.
Using 3¼mm needles and M and wrong side facing, start at inside edge of button band, pick up and K 26(27) sts up left front neck, K back neck sts, inc 8 sts evenly across them, then pick up and K 26(27) sts down right front neck, ending at inside edge of buttonhole band. 99(103) sts.
Beg with a 2nd row, work in rib as on back for 2.5cm (1in).
Change to 4mm needles and cont in rib until collar measures 9cm (3½in) from beg. Break off M, join in D and work 4 more rows, then cast off loosely in rib.

## To make up

Press work on wrong side according to instructions on ballband.
Sew in sleeves. Join side and sleeve seams. Sew down end of button band on inside. Press seams. Sew on buttons.

# 28
# CABLED COTTON

A cotton sweater to wear all year round, for the experienced knitter

**Measurements**
To fit bust 81–86(89–94)cm (32–34[35–39]in)
Length 53cm (21in)
Sleeve seam 43cm (17in)

**Materials**
Of Argyll Cotton on Cone, 2(2) 340g cones.
1 pair each of 3¼ and 4mm knitting needles.
1 cable needle.

**Tension**
30 sts and 32 rows to 10cm (4in) over pattern on 4mm needles, using yarn double.
*Note:* Yarn is used double *throughout*.

**Back**
Using 3¼mm needles, cast on 87(99) sts.
*1st row:* K1, *P1, K1, rep from * to end.
*2nd row:* P1, *K1, P1, rep from * to end.
Rep these 2 rows for 7cm (2¾in), ending with a 2nd row and inc 47 sts evenly across last row. 134(146) sts.
Change to 4mm needles and, beg with a K row, work 2 rows in st st, then cont in patt as folls:
*1st row:* K1, *sl next 3 sts on to cable needle to front of work, K3, then K3 from cable needle, K6, rep from * to last st, K1.
Beg with a P row, work 3 rows in st st.
*5th row:* K1, *K6, sl next 3 sts on to cable needle to back of work, K3, then K3 from cable needle, rep from * to last st, K1.
Beg with a P row work 3 rows in st st.

Cabled cotton

These 8 rows form the patt and are rep throughout. Cont in patt until work measures 53cm (21in) from beg, ending with a 2nd or 6th row.

*Shape shoulders*

*Next row:* Cast off 40(43) sts, K until 54(60) sts on right-hand needle, sl these sts on to a holder, change to $3\frac{1}{4}$mm needles and K to end.

Cont on these last sts, work 8 rows in garter st. Cast off.

## Front

Work as given for back until work measures 43cm (17in) from beg, ending with a 2nd or 6th patt row.

*Shape neck*
*Next row:* K58(61), turn and leave rem sts on a spare needle.
Dec one st at neck edge on every row until 40(43) sts rem, then cont without shaping until work measures 51cm (20in) from beg, ending with a 2nd or 6th row.
Change to 3¼mm needles and work 4 rows in garter st.
*Next row:* K5, K2 tog, wf, K17(18), K2 tog, wf, K to end.
Work 4 more rows in garter st. Cast off.
Return to the sts on spare needle; with right side facing sl first 18(24) sts on to a holder, rejoin yarn and K to end.
Work shaping to match first side, then cont in patt until work measures the same as back to right shoulder, ending with the same patt row.
Cast off.

## Sleeves

Using 3¼mm needles cast on 49(55) sts and work in rib as on back for 7cm (2¾in), ending with a 1st row.
*Next row*: P to end, working twice into each st. 98(110) sts.
Change to 4mm needles and cont in patt as on back until sleeve measures 43cm (17in) from beg, ending with 2nd or 6th row.
Cast off loosely.

## Neckband

Join right shoulder seam.
With 3¼mm needles and right side facing, pick up and K 6 sts along edge of buttonhole band, 33 sts down left front neck, K front neck sts, pick up and K 33 sts up right front neck, K back neck sts, then pick up and K 6 sts along edge of button band.
Work 3 rows in garter st.
*Next row:* K3, K2 tog, wf, K to end.
Work 4 more rows in garter st. Cast off.

## Buttons (Make 3)

Using 3¼mm needles cast on 6 sts and work 12 rows in st st.
Cast off. Fold work in half, P side out, and join sides. Stuff with a small amount of yarn, then join remaining side.

## To make up

Lap buttonhole band over button band and stitch at armhole edge. Sew in sleeves. Join side and sleeve seams. Sew on buttons.

29

# COTTON COOL

A lace vest top in cotton, for the average knitter

## Measurements

To fit bust 81–86(91)cm (32–34[36]in)
Length 61cm (24in)
Sleeve seam 5cm (2in)

## Materials

Of Argyll Cotton on Cone, 2 340g cones.
1 pair each of $3\frac{3}{4}$mm, $3\frac{1}{4}$mm and 4mm knitting needles.

## Tension

$22\frac{1}{2}$ sts and $25\frac{1}{2}$ rows to 10cm (4in) over pattern on 4mm needles, or size required to obtain correct tension.

*Note:* Yarn is used double *throughout.*

## Back and front

Using $3\frac{3}{4}$mm needles cast on 101(110) sts.
Work 8 rows K.
Change to 4mm needles and work in patt as follows:
*1st row:* K1, *K1, wf, K2, sl 1, K1, psso, K2 tog, K2, wf; rep from * to last st, K1 (right side).
*2nd row:* P.
*3rd row:* K1, *wf, K2, sl 1, K1, psso, K2 tog, K2, wf, K1; rep from * to last st, K1.
*4th row:* P.
These 4 rows form the pattern.
Work 44 more rows in patt.
Change to $3\frac{1}{4}$mm needles and work 12 rows K.
Change back to 4mm needles and work a further 48 rows in patt.
*Shape armholes*
Continuing to work in patt, cast off 5 sts at beg of next 2

rows, then dec 1 st at each end of next and every following row 13 times to 65(74) sts.
Work straight in patt for 5 more rows.
*Shape neck*
*Next row:* Patt 25(29) sts, turn, and leave rem sts on a spare needle.
Dec 1 st at neck edge on next 14(17) rows to 11 sts, then work straight in patt for a further 25(21) rows. Cast off.
Now slip centre 15(16) sts on to length of yarn, rejoin yarn to rem 25(29) sts, patt to end. Now shape second side to match first, reversing shapings.

Work front exactly as given for back.

Cotton cool (*opposite*)

## Sleeves

Using 3¼mm needles, cast on 65(74) sts.
Work 8 rows K.
Change to 4mm needles and work in patt as given for back and front for 8 rows.
*Shape top*
Cast off 5 sts at beg of next two rows, then dec 1 st at each end of foll 4 rows. Now dec 1 st at each end of every 4th row 8 times, then at each end of every 3rd row 3 times. Dec 1 st at each end of every row to 15(22) sts. Cast off.

## Neckband

Join right shoulder seam.
Using 3¼mm needles, pick up and K 25 sts down left side front, K up centre 15(16) sts, pick up and K 25 sts up right side front and 25 sts down right side back, K up centre back 15(16) sts, and pick up and K 25 sts up left side back. Work 4 rows K. Cast off kw loosely.

## To make up

Read and follow pressing instructions.
Join left shoulder seam. Join side seams.
Make rope belts thus:
Measure 6 lengths of yarn approx 250cm (100in); fold in two together and knot ends together. Hook knotted end over door handle or ask a friend to hold it. Pull the lengths of yarn tight and insert a pencil between the lengths of yarn at the end opposite to the knotted end. Turn the pencil clockwise until both strands are tightly twisted together,then knot together both ends of the twisted skein. Trim the end.

# 30 FLOWERBED

*(colour plates 15 and 16)*

A beautiful flower-covered cotton bedspread for a double bed

## Measurements

242cm × 216cm (7ft 11in × 7ft)

## Materials

Of Twilleys Pegasus 8 ply Cotton, 31 100g balls in main shade (2) and 2 balls in each of 10 contrast shades – red (20), pink (57), turquoise (81), yellow (6), blue (61), coral (8), pale turquoise (9), beige (4), dark blue (14) and lilac (10).
Alternatively you could use 450g of Twilleys Handicraft Cottons, HC1, D42 or C44, and dye 10 lots of 150g of these qualities in contrast shades of your choice.
1 pair of 4½mm knitting needles.

## Tension

17 sts and 26 rows to 10cm (4in) over st st on 4½mm needles, or size required to obtain correct tension.

## Instructions

Using 4½mm needles throughout, make 10 squares in each design, following Charts 1–8.
When the 80 squares have been made, join them up so that there are 10 rows of eight squares, using an edge to edge seam. Once this has been done make the edging to the quilt thus:
Using 4½mm needles and main shade, cast on 6 sts. Work in patt as follows:
*1st row:* K.
*2nd row:* K.
*3rd row:* K.
*4th row:* Cast on 3 sts, K.
*5th–7th rows:* K.

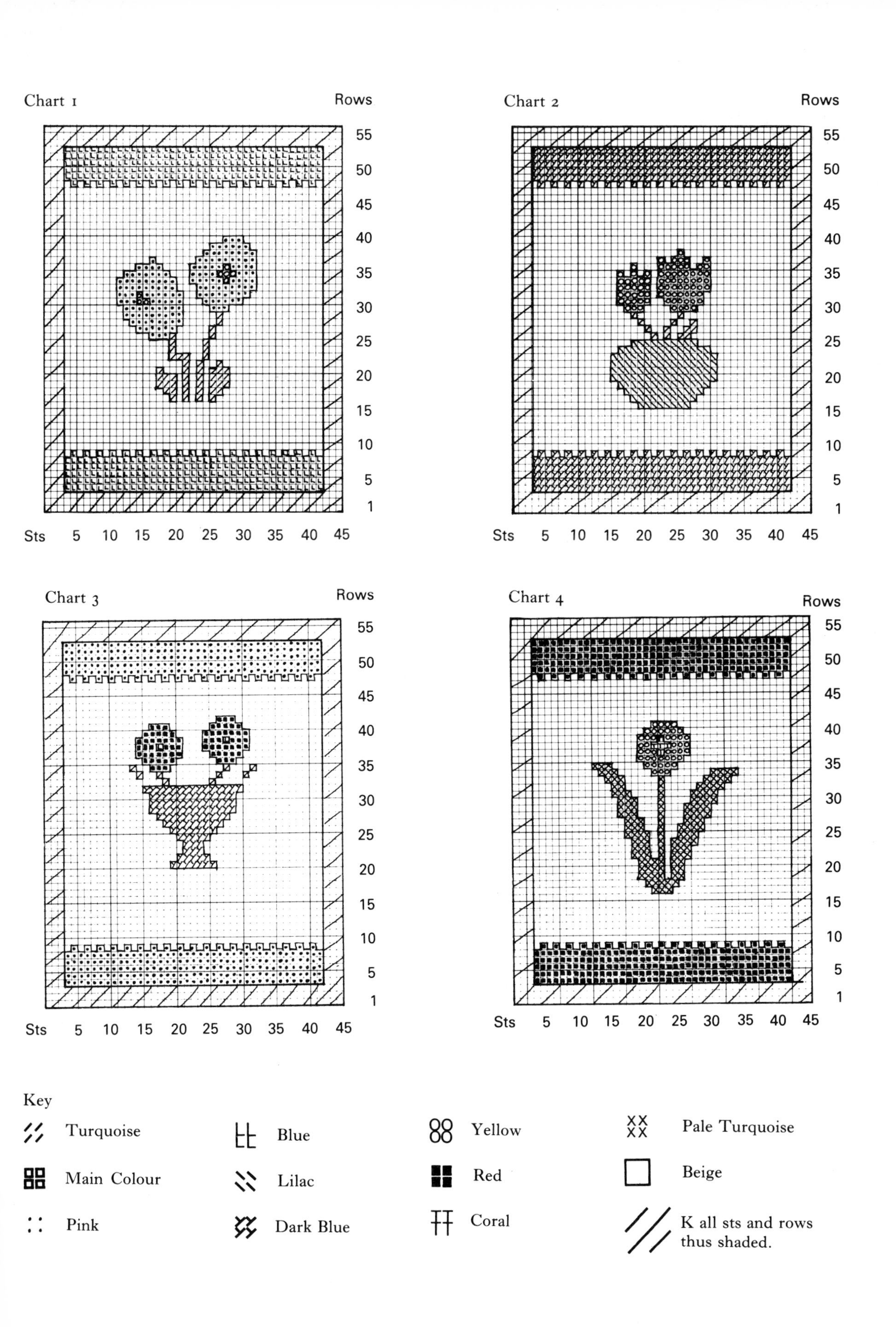

Chart 1
Rows
55
50
45
40
35
30
25
20
15
10
5
1
Sts 5 10 15 20 25 30 35 40 45
Chart 2
Rows
Sts 5 10 15 20 25 30 35 40 45
Chart 3
Rows
Sts 5 10 15 20 25 30 35 40 45
Chart 4
Rows
Sts 5 10 15 20 25 30 35 40 45
Key
Turquoise
Blue
Yellow
Pale Turquoise
Main Colour
Lilac
Red
Beige
Pink
Dark Blue
Coral
K all sts and rows thus shaded.

Chart 5

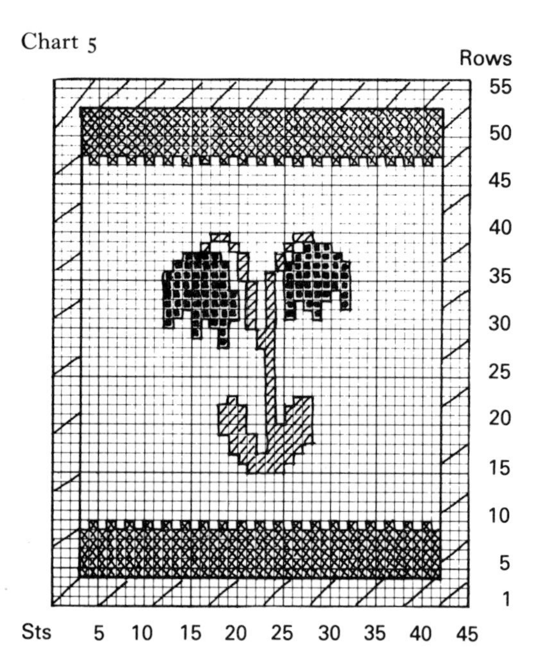


Chart 6

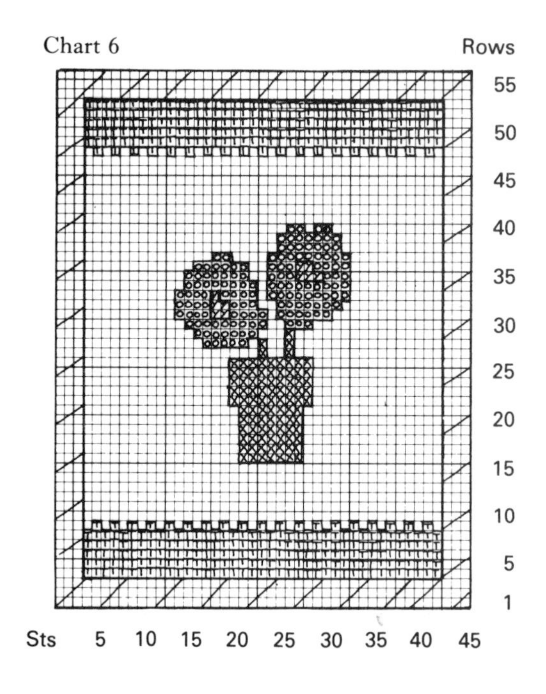


Chart 7

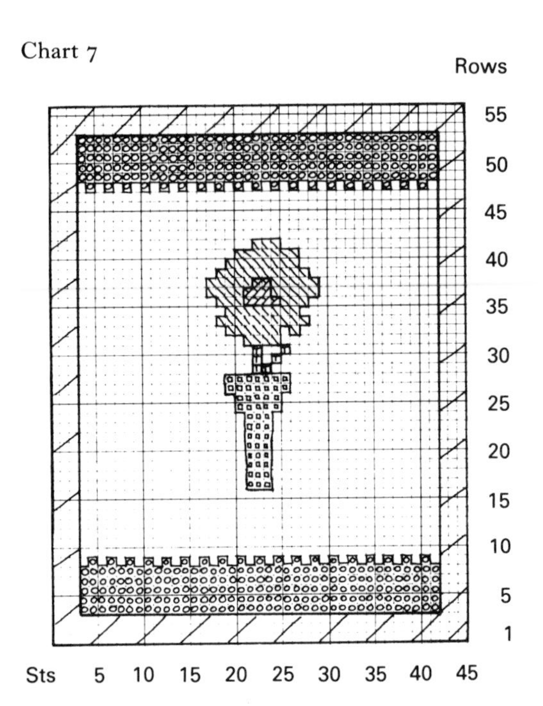


Chart 8

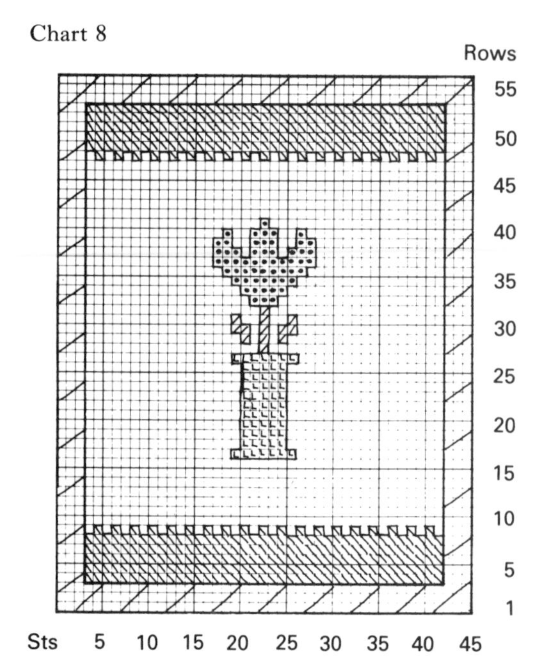

*8th row:* Cast on 3 sts, K.
*9th row:* K.
*10th row:* P.
*11th row:* K.
*12th row:* P.
*13th row:* K.
*14th row:* K.
*15th row:* K.
*16th row:* Cast off 3 sts, K.
*17th–19th rows:* K.
*20th row:* Cast off 3 sts, K.
These 20 rows form the patt. Continue working in patt until edging, when slightly stretched, fits around the quilt, gathering the edging at each corner. When the edging has been completed, stitch around the quilt.

*Note:* Twilleys recommend that this article be dry-cleaned.

# SUPPLIERS

**UK**

To obtain information about stockists in the United Kingdom, write to the following addresses:

*For Sunbeam yarns*
Richard Ingham and Co. Ltd
Crawshaw Mills
Pudsey
West Yorkshire LS28 7BS
(0532 571871)

*For Hayfield yarns*
Hayfield Textiles Ltd
Glusburn
Keighley
West Yorkshire BD20 8QP
(0532 333333)

*For Emu yarns*
Emu Wools Ltd
Leeds Road
Greengates
Bradford
West Yorkshire BD10 9TE
(9274 614031)

*For Argyll yarns*
Argyll Wools Ltd
P.P. Box 15
Priestly Mills
Pudsey
West Yorkshire LS28 9LT
(0532 574311)

*For Sirdar yarns*
Sirdar PLC
Flanshaw Lane
Alverthorpe
Wakefield
West Yorkshire WF2 9ND
(0924 371501)

*For Twilleys yarns*
H.G. Twilley Ltd
Roman Mill
Stamford
Lincolnshire PE9 1BG
(0780 52661/4)

*For Pingouin yarns*
French Wools Ltd
7–11 Lexington Street
London W1R 4BU
(01-439 8891)

*For 'Real Shetland 2 Ply Jumper yarn'*
Jamieson's Knitwear
93–95 Commercial Street
Lerwick
Shetland ZE1 0BD
(0595 3114)

*For St John's Wools yarn*
St John's Wools
P.O. Box 55
Parkside Mills
West Bowling
Bradford BD5 8DZ
(0274 729031)

## USA

Not all the yarns featured in this book are available in the USA. Unless a US stockist is listed below, readers are advised to obtain advice on suitable substitute yarns from their local yarn/craft shop.

*For Sunbeam yarns*
Grandor Industries Ltd
P.O. Box 5831
4031 Knobhill Drive
Sherman Oaks
California 91403
USA

Phillips Imports
P.O. Box 146
Port St Joe
Florida 32456
USA

*For Emu yarns*
Contact: Emu International Ltd
Leeds Road
Idle
Bradford
West Yorkshire BD10 9TE
(0274 614031)

*For Argyll yarns*
Contact Argyll Wools Ltd in the UK (address given above), who will put readers in touch with a UK mail order supplier.

*For Sirdar yarns*
Kendex Corporation
31332 Via Colinas 107
Westlake Village
California 91362
USA

*For Pingouin yarns*
Promafil Corporation
9179 Red Branch Road
Columbia
Maryland 21045
USA

*For 'Real Shetland 2 Ply Jumper yarn'*
Contact Jamieson's Knitwear in Shetland – address given above.

# CONVERSION CHARTS

**Grams to ounces** (slightly rounded – 1oz = approx. 28.35g)

| grams | 25 | 50 | 75 | 100 | 125 | 150 | 175 | 200 | 225 |
|---|---|---|---|---|---|---|---|---|---|
| ounces | 1 | $1\frac{3}{4}$ | $2\frac{3}{4}$ | $3\frac{1}{2}$ | $4\frac{1}{2}$ | $5\frac{1}{4}$ | $6\frac{1}{4}$ | 7 | 8 |
| grams | 250 | 275 | 300 | 325 | 350 | 375 | 400 | 425 | 450 |
| ounces | $8\frac{3}{4}$ | $9\frac{3}{4}$ | $10\frac{1}{2}$ | $11\frac{1}{2}$ | $12\frac{1}{4}$ | $13\frac{1}{4}$ | 14 | 15 | $15\frac{3}{4}$ |

**Centimetres to inches** (slightly rounded)

| cm | in | cm | in |
|---|---|---|---|
| 0.3 | $\frac{1}{8}$ | 48.5 | 19 |
| 0.6 | $\frac{1}{4}$ | 51 | 20 |
| 1 | $\frac{3}{8}$ | 53.5 | 21 |
| 1.3 | $\frac{1}{2}$ | 56 | 22 |
| 1.5 | $\frac{5}{8}$ | 58.5 | 23 |
| 2 | $\frac{3}{4}$ | 61 | 24 |
| 2.2 | $\frac{7}{8}$ | 63.5 | 25 |
| 2.5 | 1 | 66 | 26 |
| 3.2 | $1\frac{1}{4}$ | 68.5 | 27 |
| 3.8 | $1\frac{1}{2}$ | 71 | 28 |
| 4.5 | $1\frac{3}{4}$ | 73.5 | 29 |
| 5 | 2 | 76 | 30 |
| 6.3 | $2\frac{1}{2}$ | 78.5 | 31 |
| 7.5 | 3 | 81.5 | 32 |
| 9 | $3\frac{1}{2}$ | 84 | 33 |
| 10 | 4 | 86.5 | 34 |
| 11.5 | $4\frac{1}{2}$ | 89 | 35 |
| 12.5 | 5 | 91.5 | 36 |
| 14 | $5\frac{1}{2}$ | 94 | 37 |
| 15 | 6 | 96.5 | 38 |
| 18 | 7 | 99 | 39 |
| 20.5 | 8 | 102 | 40 |
| 23 | 9 | 104 | 41 |
| 25.5 | 10 | 107 | 42 |
| 28 | 11 | 109 | 43 |
| 30.5 | 12 | 112 | 44 |
| 33 | 13 | 115 | 45 |
| 35.5 | 14 | 117 | 46 |
| 38 | 15 | 120 | 47 |
| 40.5 | 16 | 122 | 48 |
| 43 | 17 | 125 | 49 |
| 46 | 18 | 127 | 50 |